'It's full of poetry – something to keep on the night-stand and dip in and out of when the mood takes you. There's a breath-taking amount of colour here, with the author adopting a point of view that makes what are in reality rather mundane suburbs seem like places of mystery and magic.'

www.londoneer.org

'Very engaging. Years of study and dreaming in the spare bedroom of his flat have given birth to a series of fantastic journeys...'

Observer

'Brilliantly imagined...its compelling singularity and off-message cultural engagement are things we should be profoundly thankful for.'

Time Out

Nick Papadimitriou has spent a lifetime living on the margins, walking and documenting the landscapes surrounding North London, in a study he calls Deep Topography. He was born in Finchley, Middlesex in 1958, and over the years has built up an extensive archive dedicated to this region. In 2009 John Rogers/Vanity Projects made a film about Nick titled *The London Perambulator*.

SCARP

NICK PAPADIMITRIOU

SCEPTRE

First published in Great Britain in 2012 by Sceptre
An imprint of Hodder & Stoughton
An Hachette UK company

First published in paperback in 2013

2

A CIP catalogue record for this title is available from the British Library.

ISBN 978 1 444 72339 7

Typeset by Hewer Text UK Ltd, Edinburgh
Printed and bound by Clays Ltd, St Ives plc

Supported using public funding by the National
Lottery through Arts Council England.

Hodder & Stoughton policy is to use papers that are natural, renewable
and recyclable products and made from wood grown in sustainable
forests. The logging and manufacturing processes are expected to
conform to the environmental regulations of the country of origin.

Hodder & Stoughton Ltd
338 Euston Road
London NW1 3BH

www.sceptrebooks.co.uk

For Rehana and Bella.
With special thanks to
Will Self and John Rogers.

CONTENTS

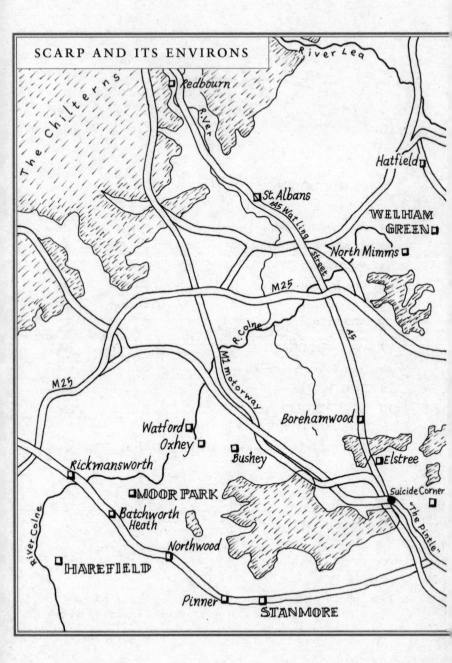

SCARP AND ITS ENVIRONS

The Chilterns

River Lea

Redbourn

R. Ver

Hatfield

St. Albans

A5 Watling Street

WELHAM GREEN

North Mimms

M 25

R. Colne

A5

M1 motorway

M25

Borehamwood

Watford

Oxhey

Bushey

Elstree

Rickmansworth

MOOR PARK

Suicide Corner

River Colne

Batchworth Heath

"The Pintle"

Northwood

HAREFIELD

Pinner

STANMORE

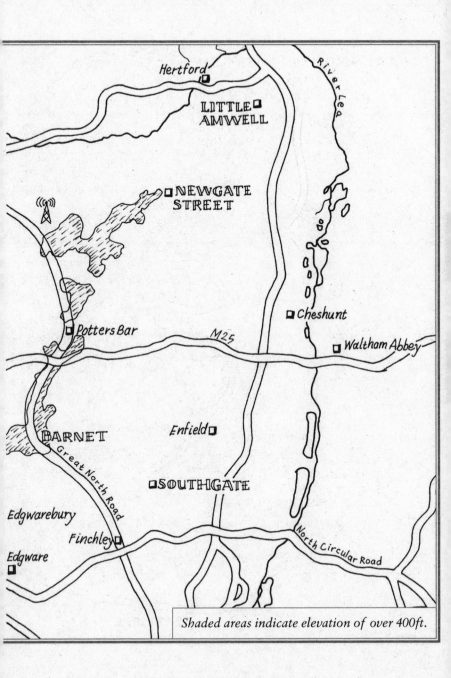

INTRODUCTION

A vast yet seemingly invisible presence hovers over the northern suburbs of London. Screened from the consciousness of the city dweller by the pressures of the day-to-day, by self-concern and an inward-looking and anthropocentric culture, the North Middlesex/South Hertfordshire escarpment – or Scarp as I prefer to call it – broods and waits.

On summer evenings – when the sun sets furthest north – Scarp casts its shadow over the car-cluttered roads and sedate closes that break against its southern rim. Winter brings the sound of water gushing below low points in the suburban streets and shopping parades as the streams that rise on Scarp swell and are channelled beneath Edgware, Pinner or Ruislip and flow towards their confluence with two broader rivers which embrace London's northern margins, the Lea and Colne.

I, too, flow downhill through time and distance from some as yet undiscovered point of origin on Scarp, and the growing awareness of this builds in me a desire to return. As I sip my Polish-style coffee at day's end and stare out through my high-rise kitchen window at the distant green and brown mass slumped like a somnolent reptile across the landscape, I realise yet again that my destiny is bound up with Scarp.

When the caffeine hits, I leave the bills, the money pressures and the electronic chaff behind me, and burst through the window and over the cars parked far below. I surge across the rooftops of Hendon and Edgware and above the A roads, retail centres and white suburbs, as I rise above Scarp's summit. Descending, I pass through soft rippling grass roots and sandy topsoil. I become the stratum of gravels surfacing on a hill track after heavy rain, patches of warmth sliding over stiff clay and minuscule variations in the angle of surface slope by concrete tracks I walked last week, last decade, last century, and always alone.

And it is there, on long walks over the years, that voices come to me as I traipse across fields, cut through woods between riding schools and mean farms. A sense of lives real and imagined rises from the steel streams of cars passing endlessly along motorway cuttings, and gazes from the trains that curve through Scarp's lower levels at Edgwarebury or Carpender's Park.

I think also of the lives of birds, mammals, and insects, those sentient beings whose undervalued and endangered domain of coppice and spinney, burnt-out car and fly-tipped mound interpenetrates the human world.

Scarp, taken from west to east, rises just south of Harefield, on the Middlesex–Hertfordshire border, crosses remote Batchworth Heath and then runs via Moor Park and Oxhey Wood to Bushey. From there it heads eastwards through to Stanmore and then – after a dip that accommodates the M1 motorway – rises again to Elstree. And further east, the ridge takes in High Barnet and Hadley, widening considerably north of the former towards Ridge and North Mimms. The eastern edge of Scarp curves north and then north-east, following the river Lea upstream into Hertfordshire, until it diminishes in height in the region of Hertford and Great Amwell. Scarp's northern slope faces onto the Hertfordshire plain towards St Albans and Hatfield, a land broken by the river valleys of the Lea and Colne. The Chiltern range is clearly visible from many points, particularly in Scarp's western sector. Southwards, Scarp gazes loweringly upon London and across to the North Downs and Kentish Hills on the far side of the Thames basin.

Several notable spurs protrude north and southwards from various points along the main escarpment: the long spits of high ground forming Totteridge and Mill Hill both originate in the region of Moat Mount, source of the river Brent, in the London Borough of Barnet. Over on the north side of the ridge an elongated plateau juts out from Borehamwood in the direction of Well End, Shenleybury and the lost Hertfordshire manor of Titburst. Here the sources of the Catharine Bourne and an unnamed tributary of the Tykes Water flow east and west respectively. A further northward-pointing plateau takes in South and North Mimms before receding in height towards the river Colne.

Despite being some seventeen miles from east to west and attaining in excess of 400 feet above sea level in places, Scarp is seldom commented upon by either topographers or psycho-geographers, and seemingly possesses no cultural currency. Sliced by railways and motorways, topped by old roads running its length, repeatedly scarred in the name of civic utility, yet never acknowledged openly as possessing a coherent identity, Scarp nevertheless persists in the infrastructural unconscious of the northern reaches of the city.

Scarp can be seen from numerous points in the London area. A large section taking in Edgwarebury, Deacons Hill and Great Stanmore is clearly visible from the Hampstead Heath extension; the meadows on the western slope of Harrow-on-the-Hill look out towards Harrow Weald Common and Pinner Hill; elongated promontories jut out from Scarp into the northern suburbs of London, reaching as far south as Southgate and the curious tongue of high ground at Canons Park in Little Stanmore. North London's sewage system is aligned with the rivers running off Scarp – our arterial roads follow the river valleys created by the confluence of these streams and also provide the framework for the trunk sewers serving north London and south Hertfordshire. There is an irony here, because the major roads that cut through or run alongside Scarp rose out of a need to accommodate the motor cars that replaced London's horses, animals that were fed by fodder grown on Scarp, at one time known as 'the Hay Country'. The utilities we most take for granted – macro-engineered indicators of our modernity and efficiency – are thus inextricably bound up with Scarp's existence.

Scarp has been a presence in the back of my mind from my earliest days. I have a memory, dating from the age of about six, of accompanying my father to a wedding in Burnt Oak, a small suburb of London situated on the A5 Watling Street. After the vows were taken and the confetti thrown, the newlyweds departed by Routemaster while I sat on the wall outside the register office and stared northwards along the dead straight road towards the dark belt of land that rose above the roofs of Edgware a mile or so distant. A modern white multi-storey office block in Station Road and a clutch of high-rises further off were rendered insignificant against the visual backdrop of this band of high land. I remember that now, as I look out my kitchen window and reach for my old Bartholomew's maps of Middlesex and Hertfordshire, check once again the contour lines, river routes and names of estates on Scarp, and locate myself within the larger context, the broad sweep of the land I inhabit.

Later, playing truant one day in my teens – it must have been around July 1972 – I walked, for reasons that no longer matter, from Finchley, where I lived with my dad and brother, to Mill Hill, a seeming paradise of weatherboard cottages and mock-baronial mansions perched on high ground on London's margins. The sky unexpectedly darkened and then pelted down all that afternoon, the warm, heavy, blood-scented rain-drops speckling and then blackening the pavement in seconds and forcing me to shelter in a ramshackle barn on the edge of the green belt. Curled in the hay to preserve heat, my atten-tion was drawn towards the black hills that loomed threaten-ingly over the bungalow belt and the orange-lit by-pass in the middle distance. The dim afternoon light foreshortened Scarp's contours, emphasising its towering presence: something unset-tling and dangerous lurked in those hills and stared down on my small life. I fell asleep, exhausted by the effort of trying to accommodate this glowering thing, waking later for the long, damp walk home.

Later still, as a young man in my twenties in the early 1980s, my internal map of London – a city of arty cafés, doomed romances and outlandish hairstyles – was ripped apart following an afternoon I spent in Great Stanmore in order to study the wild flowers in which I had begun to take an interest. A Middlesex flora that I'd recently bought listed the heath land adjacent to the mansion of Bentley Priory as a good place to find various ferns, so that day I took the Underground to the end of the new Jubilee Line, and headed off up steep streets towards the grand eighteenth-century house. Bentley Priory is Middlesex's highest point and – though I didn't think of it as such at the time – part of Scarp. As I worked my way along the security fences surrounding the house and onto the ridge behind, a new and destabilising view of the city I thought I knew so well opened up below me. The land dropped steeply southwards and I found myself staring across a deep void, my eyes rolling over the Thames basin towards the skyscrapers at Croydon, fifteen miles distant. The distinctively 1930s and sharp-edged St Helier's Hospital in Carshalton was diminished by distance to a white smudge against the blue of the North Downs and further off – just visible through the Dorking Gap – were other hills, their vague grey forms distant and unsettling reminders that the life I was trying to shape for myself was rooted in a larger matrix. My immediate concerns – a romantic rejection delivered by post that morning, and my worries about an expanding bald patch – were suddenly as nothing, and were transcended as my senses were drawn beyond the distant downs into clouds, sunlight and a sense of cold grey oceans. It was my first direct encounter with Scarp as an agent of consciousness expansion, my first intimate exposure to its perception-altering power.

This experience triggered in me a desire to consciously explore my region, initially as a lifestyle choice, and eventually as the basis of an ill-defined philosophical inquiry. Over the next few years I occasionally visited Scarp, though I as yet had no sense of it as an entity. My early walks were based on London Transport walking guides and were invariably orientated towards the classic landscapes of the Chilterns, but these slowly gave way to walks closer to my home in Childs Hill, north London. *Discovering Country Walks in North London*, a much-overlooked book written by Merry Lundow in the mid-1970s, introduced me to the Edgwarebury uplands. Here, where old Edgwarebury Lane climbs from the Watford by-pass to a belt of countryside intersected by the M1 motorway and the railway to Northamptonshire, I was greeted with views across to Harrow-on-the Hill, Horsendon Hill, and the Hampstead *petit massif*.

On the valley floor below I could see the houses, roads and factories of Edgware, Colindale and West Hendon. These suburbs – rendered tiny from my newly discovered viewpoint – were the stage set for my human-scale encounters, little dramas designed to fit within the lounge, the coffee shop and the bedroom. The experience widened my consciousness; now something larger and older, less crammed with my petty concerns looked out through my eyes and wondered at the time I routinely wasted.

Walks undertaken over the next few months in the area of Potters Bar and South Mimms lifted me into new landscapes, complex reminders of how circumscribed my usual experience was. As I headed north along the Great North Road from High Barnet, I sensed I was straying further from my habitual world. To the east the view was of a deep river gully that climbed to high land on its opposite side, to what I now know as Foxhole Hill, Plumridge, and the spur that forms the basis for the Ridgeway, the road connecting Enfield to the M25. As the fields gave way to the first houses of Potters Bar I was pulled free of the gravity that had previously bound me to my everyday life. Further off still, the land rose to the Barvins, Northaw and the high ground around Newgate Street but of these, I as yet knew nothing.

As I began to learn the basic outline of these topographic details and hold them in my mind, my internal balance would oscillate between the ego's surrender in the face of a larger entity – the land that contained me – and a desire to gain ownership and mastery of that same entity through cultural production. The idea grew that there was a new form of prose or poetry waiting to be invented, a form of writing sufficient for the purpose of capturing the essence of the broader framework to which I had surrendered, a form that would allow me to re-create the voices and experiences of those Scarp dwellers who came before me as a counterpoint to my own.

Voices other than the merely historic surfaced on my walks: the groaning of South London villains entombed in motorway bridges; women long dead glimpsed with the inner eye when I stared through windows into warm-lit rooms passed on freezing afternoons; garish tales told by beings that confounded accepted notions of time; the outrage of mossy elementals lingering in relic woodlands. Finally there was another presence that shadowed me wherever I went. This one spoke with my own voice, whispering endlessly of a journey I'd made into another unacknowledged aspect of the region several years earlier, and seeking to make sense of that voyage of the damned in the light of what I – or rather, *we* – now knew.

The epiphany that led to the writing of this book finally occurred in August 2009, after twenty years of walking. That Saturday I left Oakwood Underground Station and headed off through suburban streets towards the green belt country of Enfield Chase. I wanted to experience step by step the detailed transition from the margins of north London to something approaching actual countryside. As I reached the point where houses finally ended and dropped down into the lush valley of the Salmon Brook I found myself looking over to the west in order to gain a glimpse of the stream's source at a small triangle of emergent woodland named Spoilbank Wood. In my mind I linked the wood with points further west such as Dancer's Hill and Welham Green, places walked through repeatedly over the past few years in wildly varying weather conditions. And reaching out from these places in turn, my thoughts extended to further cardinal points in the broader landscape until a large section of its component features was laid out in my mind like a map. I knew, for instance, that the Salmon Brook takes further water from two streams, the Leeging Beech Gutter and the Merryhills Brook, both of which surface on the eastern edge of a belt of high ground that juts out southwards from the farm country at Ferny Hill, midway between High Barnet and Enfield Town. However, the details didn't matter so much as the overall vision, the sense of otherwise disparate elements being bound together in one larger presence.

As I approached the stream at the bottom of the valley I could feel the breadth of knowledge I'd gained over the years of walking burst through the strictures placed on me by the daily requirements of living. It was as if the landscape itself was flooding into the front of my mind. I was in a state of ecstatic union with the Middlesex–Hertfordshire borderlands.

Later, I climbed onto a bald height at Holy Hill Farm and looked eastwards to the distant blackness of Epping Forest in Essex. I crossed a footbridge over the M25 motorway and sat down on a mossy tree stump to smoke a roll-up, the sound of the traffic hissing in my ears. And it was then that I apprehended that the long ridge of land beneath my feet had never been properly written about. As I smoked, I thought about my slow exposure to Scarp and all the years it had taken me to understand that the apparently unconnected places I had walked through, like Harefield, Stanmore and Barvin Hill, in fact shared a deep connecting substratum, the underlying belt of high ground on which they were situated.

This book is neither a detailed geographical and historical survey, nor a wholesome itinerary of 'fine' places within easy reach of the metropolis written for the benefit of the casual walker: there are plenty of such books already in print. It is, rather, an inquiry undertaken in order to systematically 'feel out' the presence of my subject matter as it brushes against the consciousness. After an initial encounter at the centre of Scarp, we'll begin in Harefield in the west, and gradually move eastwards. Throughout, I will reconstruct the ghostly voices I hear while walking on Scarp in an attempt to relate my own story to theirs, to locate my own voice and sensations in the ones that came before me – whether those of a murderer, an animal, a deceived young woman, a master botanist, or any of the other myriad layers of experience that distil over the centuries to create regional memory. The deeper implication is that the world that confronts us through our immediate surroundings is alive and intrinsically valuable in ways not amenable to instrumental reason or economic reductionism.

A note on parameters
I undertook something like thirty walks during the summer of 2011 in preparation for this book. The walks varied between three and twelve miles and served to sharpen my focus on the subject covered here. I wanted to understand the overall structure of Scarp, the transition between its component parts, where and how it begins. As I trudged across fields, through hostile-seeming suburbs and beneath A roads I came to understand that in some respects Scarp was a fiction.

In particular, I had to make some arbitrary decisions as to what aspects of the general belt of high ground to the north of London could be considered to be integral parts of Scarp. I had no fixed notions of what height above sea level would be considered sufficient to allow an area to be included in the project. This was partly because the numerous maps of the borderlands between Herts and Middlesex I have in my possession follow widely differing conventions with regard to how they colour code gradations of height. For instance, one old map, dating from the 1920s and titled *Bartholomew's North London Roads and Countryside* depicted all land above 200 feet in a uniform light brown. This provided a picture of Scarp's dramatic sweep across (what would in a few years be) the northern suburbs. However, if I were simply to take the map colouring as my guide I would be forced to stray far south from my chosen field and include not only Finchley, mounted high on its platform of boulder clays, but also the gravels and sands of the Hampstead and Harrow massifs. This I did not want to do as it drew the focus of this book away from my central argument: that a significant land feature lies unacknowledged at London's doorstep. I decided therefore to ignore these places.

However, the relatively low land between Pinner Hill and Harrow Weald *is* included in this work, despite its being somewhat lower in height than either Finchley or Hampstead. To my mind, this dip in the hills taking in Hatch End and the South Oxhey colony is a component part of Scarp, whereas the wealthy and languid suburbs mentioned in the previous paragraph most definitely are not.

I will make frequent reference in this work to the County of Middlesex. This 'Cinderella of counties' has been badly treated by history: the Local Government Act of 1888 resulted in the transfer of fifty-one square miles of eastern Middlesex to the newly formed County of London. The following year Monken Hadley and East Barnet (formerly in the Middlesex Hundred of Edmonton) were absorbed into Hertfordshire. Finally, in April 1965 the administration of Middlesex was handed over to a group of London boroughs, the County Council was dissolved and Middlesex disappeared to all intents and purposes – today only a cricket team, a county court, a university and a few postal addresses remain to remind us of what has been.

Nevertheless, to my mind, the county's time-honoured presence in the region, despite its eventual dissolution, carries with it a greater weight than the existence of London's inward-looking and increasingly profit-minded northern boroughs. Perhaps also I'm seeking to foreground a sense of historic continuity, a fixity and frame of reference akin to the botanist Hewett Cottrell Watson's notion of the biological vice-counties, a series of geographical divisions used for the purposes of biological recording and other scientific data-gathering, as outlined in his *Cybele Britannica* of 1852.

We lock together and become woodlands and river valleys. We flow, an iron-rusted streamlet, into broad alluvial marshlands. We are plant successions and the spoor of animals, sour green berries and clicking insects in late summer grass. Time hangs over the murmuring land as we move on to endings at oceans, at salt spray and feather-clad wildness.

And afterwards there is the greasy kitchen and the view from the window across car parks, over shopping complexes and streets packed with the minds of strangers. There is the distant high ground running across the window's frame; a belt of land lit yellow-green or umber or dark blue: Scarp.

1

SUICIDE CORNER

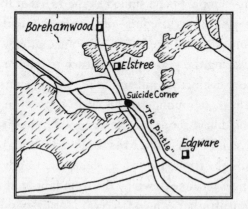

AUBURN-HAIRED AND ELFIN-FACED, MISS Borehamwood 1954 was picked up at eight o'clock at her house in Elstree by her fiancé William McGrath. After a quick spin in McGrath's white MG Midget to St Albans where they had dinner, the couple set off south, car roof down on the hot June evening, heading for Edgware and the cinema. As they passed over Elstree Hill, Sheila Margaret Lomath and William McGrath discussed plans for their wedding day. Everything was arranged, the service at St Nicholas's church, Elstree, to be followed by a reception at the Orchard Restaurant in Mill Hill. The honeymoon would be spent touring France, the new

Mr and Mrs McGrath (plus MG Midget) taking the Silver City cross-channel air ferry from Lydd in Kent to Dunkirk. As they shouted to one another over the engine noise, the evening air hitting their faces, they crossed Brockley Hill, swung onto the sleek and modern A41 Edgware Way and plummeted down off the ridge at 70 mph. Sheila smiled as she gazed at the curve of street lamps marking the course of the arterial road up ahead; in her beautiful mind the chain of orange globes became a necklace bearing the years to come, each jewel-like soda-light a rich season, distinct yet integral to the shaping pattern of her life. William merely pondered his luck: to wed an ex-beauty queen – who'd have thought it? It was good to be alive in 1958.

Forty-five minutes later Miss Borehamwood 1954 is no more. While the firemen cut her decapitated body free from the smoking wreckage down by the roundabout at Newlands Corner, the traffic backs up on the two-lane by-pass all the way to Five Ways Corner in Hendon, all the way to The Spider's Web Motel near Watford. Faces stare from the windows of the new tower blocks in the Spur Road estate as an ambulance speeds off, carrying a critically injured McGrath to Edgware General Hospital. A *Hendon Times* reporter licks his pencil before asking a copper for inside information while Public Carriage officers from Scotland Yard standing in their Macintoshes by the other vehicle involved in the crash – a six-ton British Road Services truck carrying fruit down from Leyland in Lancashire – photograph the silvery skid-marks of the MG Midget's final moments. The reporter shakes his head woefully: this is just the latest fatality in a year that has seen Edgware's so-called 'mile of death' truly earning its title.

1958 opened with a bang on 6 January when a car driven by Mr Sidney Thomas Davies, sixty-nine, collided with a bus at the junction of the A41 and Station Road, Hendon. Mr Davies was thrown through the car windscreen and suffered fatal injuries, including multiple fractures to his skull. He had been driving his family back to their home in Watford from a day out in London's West End when the accident occurred. His son, recording engineer Peter Thomas Davies, later described the sound of the impact as 'the loudest noise I ever heard'. A fatality left unrecorded at the subsequent coroner's inquiry was Mrs Davies' poodle, Bon-Bon, left to lie bleeding to death in the glass-strewn gutter outside the local branch of the National Provincial Bank.

Less than a week later, Mr Wilfred Fienburgh, thirty-seven, Labour MP for Islington North, died instantly after his car mounted the pavement and hit a concrete street lamp near Apex Corner, the junction of the Watford by-pass and Barnet Way. Mr Fienburgh was returning to his flat in Hemel Hempstead following a day spent surveying housing conditions in Bethnal Green. Friends later described how he had seemed pale and tired on the day of his death. This was due to a sleepless night brought on by the disruptive effect of a hacking cough.

In May three passengers alighting from a 113 bus – Mark Cohen, fifty-six; Mrs Dorothy Fawcett, sixty-seven; and her daughter, Yvonne Williams, forty – were killed after an estate car ploughed into them at the bus-stop by the junction of the

A41 and Tithe Walk, Mill Hill. The driver – a twenty-one-year-old man from Elstree – lost control of his vehicle as the result of a sudden puncture caused by a one-and-a-half inch wood-screw later found embedded in the car's rear off-side tyre.

As Sheila Lomath's body is wheeled towards a waiting ambulance, a brown rat emerges from the roadside herbage and rummages in a shopping bag dumped by a chipped concrete bollard before dragging a greyed sliver of ox-tail onto the York paving. Unperturbed by the arc lamps and the purring fire engines, it hunches over its find. Overhead, on a premoulded concrete street lamp, a crow perches and mocks the event taking place beneath. After the rat has disappeared into the nettles the bird drops heavily and takes his turn. Pulling cold spaghetti from one of the bags, he grips the slimy stringy stuff with his right claw, pinning it to the paving as he leans forward and down to take his fill. Further along the pavement flaccid mauve mallows lie strewn across the hot granite of the road's edge. Nearby, behind a mound of gravel topped by scentless mayweed and white horseradish, pretty yellow Johnny-Go-to-Bed-at-Noon stands wrapped in his green gown, well and truly asleep. As a crane flips the burnt-out MG Midget the right way up, the flowers are swayed by a stirring of cool air permeated with the scent of hay, fresh-blown over Scarp from the distant Chiltern Hills. The world has not ended with the tragedy at Newlands Corner.

Meanwhile, a mile uphill at Brockley Grange Farm, where the A41 straddles Scarp at Suicide Corner before descending into Hertfordshire, a dream of motorways takes shape in the mind of a civil engineer working for the transport ministry who, though eyeing the scraggy wood just to the north of the farmhouse, sees only camber, curve and how best to extend the planned M1 extension over this high ground from its present terminus. Momentarily distracted from his plans by the chirring of some unnameable night bird, he looks eastwards across the brightly lit Edgware Way, towards the high ground at Edgwarebury. Perhaps moved by some spontaneous memory of childhood holidays spent in the New Forest, his imagination lingers in the woods and fields like a slowly drifting plant community and then dissolves into ditches lined with black waterlogged leaves – a residue of previous summers – and the ghosts of dead insects. The same breeze from the Chilterns that shook the wild flowers further down the hill ruffles the grass at the civil engineer's feet and, feeling suddenly cold, he decides to leave. Turning, he mounts his motor scooter and heads off home for creamed tomato soup and beans on toast. His rear light soon merges into the molten red stream marking the northbound evening traffic, now eased with Sheila Lomath's removal.

Half a century on and the wood at Brockley Grange Farm is home to neither badger nor brook. A swirling frenzy of feed roads – drivers farting in their Range Rovers, Smart cars steered by nose-picking charity fundraisers, air fresheners swinging endlessly in windscreens – drowns out a rumour of Boudicca, Queen of the Iceni, supposedly buried on Stanmore Common just to the west, behind the Royal National Orthopaedic Hospital where Sheila Lomath's body rested after her own last journey via Verulam.

The orthopaedic hospital is located on a broad plateau topping Brockley Hill. According to the black circular plaque mounted on the wall of the barge-boarded lodge house by its entrance, the hospital was established in 1921 to provide 'a cure for crippled children'. Now the grounds are packed with stream-lined new medical and administrative units slowly displacing the mansard-roofed brick nursing school, the wartime utility blocks. All burnished metal façade with pastel-coloured inlaid panels, these smoke-free, humming health factories are moni-tored closely for acceptable levels of appropriate behaviour and cross-cultural inclusiveness.

As the new arrives and is accommodated, the old is neglected, abandoned and then quietly killed off. There is a derelict 1920s fever ward standing near the western edge of the hospital grounds between the 1970s nurses' flats and the obelisk cele-brating the battle supposedly fought here between the Romans and the Catuvellauni in 54 BC. It is a long, low brick structure, with sun-bleached awnings hanging in rags from a steel frame mounted above its breeze-blocked entrance, and an off-white mock bell tower perched on its pantiled roof.

With its boarded-up windows and padlocked doors, the old fever ward seems to have given up and turned its face from the world, as if wounded by some heart-shattering betrayal. There is a way inside though, via a twisted and wrenched delivery hatch located at the building's rear. It is a portal through to a cham-ber of imagined memory buried deep in the wet winter land-scape. Discarded hospital trolleys, oxygen cylinders, prosthetic limbs and NHS-issue beds and mattresses lie stacked or scattered throughout the building's dark interior. Broad corridors recede to mind-traces of a matron clutching thank-you letters 1967, to oranges and bunches of grapes in brown paper bags 1977, and to the long slow haul of faceless patients towards health or otherwise. The sense of something precious – a soft vulnerable humanity interwoven with businesslike yet compassionate expertise – hovers in the silences, sweeping across the dusty cobwebbed surfaces of the medical implements and through the dormitories with their drained radiators and scratched linoleum floors. There is a brushing of dead spikes of buddleia against steel-framed windows. Pigeons scratch and momentarily flutter as they shift on their perches in the roof. These are the whispers of deep-time.

Just to the north of the paediatrics block – down some concrete steps into a shallow valley, and past the ruins of the home-farm – a small tear-shaped pool of clear water marks the issuing of a stream from beneath the Bagshot sands capping Brockley Hill. The water fills a natural basin worn into the surface of the London clay before brimming over and trickling downhill to pass into Hertfordshire. It is one of the sources of the Tykes Water, the main feeder of the Aldenham Reservoir a mile to the north. Its current carries off the dead MP, the ex-beauty queen, the brown rat, the haggard fever patients sweating in their striped pyjamas. The black leaves flow like a plague of mice across the windy earth. The Internet will bear no trace of them. But Scarp sees it all.

I was born in 1958 into a world that, despite its best efforts, still had the war hanging over its shoulder. The conventional

Edwardian suburb in which my family lived tried hard to forget the recent fighting, the hunger and the sacrifices made, but these lingered on in the haggard faces of my teachers and in the brick bomb shelters behind Simms' Motor Units, where my father worked. The fear of war could still be heard in the occasional public testing of air-raid sirens, a panic-edged warbling that invoked a collective memory of Heinkels or Dorniers throbbing over the suburbs and cold needles of light piercing the night sky. The shock waves seemed to recede sometime in the mid-1960s, to be replaced by TVs, flared purple trouser suits and more and more parked cars. Now we lived – or so I was assured by my parents and *Blue Peter* – in an age of decency and safety. However, I never quite believed this and sensed that the dignified rows of houses in my road, with their colourful and welcoming front doors and gaily patterned window sashes, were conspiring to create an illusion of permanence. Their apparent fixity seemed to me to be a lie, the momentary dream of a nameless and ultimately vindictive earth god.

From an early age I used walking as an instrument of research, the aim being to step straight through the cracks in the apparent world, the shared beliefs of my little electrically lit Middlesex colony. My plastic Daleks and Airfix confederate infantry; my sombre parents, trying hard; the kind school with its gaily coloured wall paintings, its milk and biscuits freely given: all these I left behind when I first explored the alley two houses down. This led, via dustbins and strewn cinders, to where our happy houses mutated into unadorned cliff-faces of brown brick permanently deprived of sunlight.

Set in honeycombed concrete at the alley's lowest point there was a metal plate. When I bent down and placed my ear to it I heard indecipherable groans and shrieks rising from some sinister place located deep beneath our front gardens, our ornate wrought-iron gates and tarpaulined Morris Minors. The alley ended at a zone fenced with green railings containing a large electricity substation. Giant orange fish swirled silently in a broad cooling lagoon visible behind the blockhouses and Lombardy poplars; the substation, with its humming serious-ness, its insulation porcelains and high-tension cables, seemed to be a place of unheeded urgency and danger.

The manhole covers, stern-faced backs of houses and lank weeds spoke a different language from the one used by the adults who surrounded me in my daily life: they challenged the self-assuming certainty of the events played out in the sitting room at home or on the screen of the TV set that had recently arrived. They were doorways through to something larger, older and darker that lurked behind the narratives of our home lives – something that in my imagination took the form of a gnarled and ancient man made of moss, mud and wood who visited us at night, staring fiercely through the windows as we watched *Criss-Cross Quiz*.

But it was an in-out on-off sort of consciousness, this passing below the everyday scheme of things. A new series of *Doctor Who*; the packs of American Civil War cards I bought from the local sweet shop; days out to Hampstead Heath with the family that lived opposite – these served to slot me back into my place in the shared community.

In the early 1970s I was introduced to a different sort of darkness, another unmapped region. The cataclysm of my parents' failed marriage, which culminated in my mother's bruised and defeated departure from home, seemed to my mind to correspond somehow with the bearded and slovenly people appearing on the TV or seen on the street. Gone was the cartoon innocence, the smooth-chinned 1960s hero – invariably an American – and the optimism manifest in jelly beans and Supercar. Now Simon Dee was losing it – all loon pants and jeering lips – and the clean-cut beat groups of yesteryear became serious bands, angrily sporting patch-jeans and lanky hair. Now the boys from Alder School rolled us in nettles; now Mrs Frobisher flashed her knickers as she bent over the school desk in front with her mini-dress riding high. There were nauseatingly long runs along the footpath by the North Circular Road courtesy of a sports teacher who terrified me with his slipper; there was a freezing-cold home and my dad spitting and pissing into a yellow plastic bucket as he died a day at a time from Guards filter tips while breathlessly intoning 'the bitch, the bitch'. There were also the tough boys with cropped hair and tie-dyed T-shirts who hung around the chip shop on Long Lane, their boots – ox-bloodied for action – twisting out smouldering fag butts.

Later, more mobile and intent on escaping the gladiator ring of my secondary school's fully equipped gym, I bunked off, forsaking my free school dinners for a little peace and safety. This was a perilous decision, one made in desperation. The danger came not from strange men I might meet and had been warned about but from the police or from the 'greenies' – the London Borough of Barnet vans that seemed to be everywhere in those days – or from running into either a teacher or, worst of all, my dad.

The winter of 1970–71 saw me hiding out during school hours in a patch of wasteland situated between the back gardens of the houses on Glebe Road and the North Circular Road. It was a low-lying acre or so full of interesting junk – rusting cogs and sprockets, scorched pages from 1950s boys' annuals, a patched and leaking space-hopper – that rose through twisted ivy and sycamore at its border to meet the edge of the arterial road. All day the traffic droned past as I hunkered down into a little shack I'd made from planks, mildewed tarpaulin and a small septic tank. Here I would wait out the long freezing hours until fading light and schoolkids passing along the alley close by told me I could safely return home.

The wasteland was a good place to experiment with fire. I rifled the garden sheds of the houses on Glebe Road for methylated spirits and other flammables. Stacks of timber, the dried-out stems of summer's weeds, old newspapers – homes for earwigs and harvestmen – all were utilised. The resulting blaze kept me warm during the cold days.

The best thing about this tiny province of mine was 'the sewer', a five-foot-high concrete-covered pipe that ran the length of the wasteland in parallel with the North Circular. The sewer spoke of hidden dimensions, of the smug suburb's need to accommodate mysterious processes, ones that could be directed to some degree but could never be wished away.

Halfway along the pipe was a brick inspection chamber topped by a manhole plate inscribed FUDC (Finchley Urban District Council). Here I would sit and survey my lands while bands of black smoke rose from burning tins of paint and wound through the dense brambles. It was my throne and watch-tower combined, this squat and sinister block, a central clearing house for the processing of information – mutterings and murmurings – that seemed to be channelled through the pipe.

When the cold got to be too much I would walk. Perhaps eastwards into the Rough Lots, a swampy area frequented by odd men, that was once part of Finchley Common. It was here in 1970, during a dustmen's strike, that I set fire to piles of household waste in the borough's dust destructor. Alarmed by the intensity of the resulting inferno I fled through the woods, past stinking ponds and men languidly smoking by the gents' lavatory. I was convinced that all police units would be on to me immediately and expected to hit the Great North Road only to see a blue Rover pull up and some copper scratching his arse as he climbed out to arrest me. Then it would be leather car seats and stony-faced policemen while East Finchley sped past. Then it would be sweet tea and a chain-smoking civilian typist tapping away on her typewriter as I systematically incriminated myself.

My home was another cold and hungry wasteland. Every evening I returned to the smoke-damaged kitchen – resulting from a fire I'd lit in 1966 – to rummage about in the dark cellar where we stored the china plates and broken vacuum cleaners, the now unused Christmas decorations, of my earliest life.

Perhaps I thought that somewhere down there – hidden in the coal dust or in one of the tobacco tins packed with bent nails and screws – I would find a key to some other place, some other life.

My dad was a flat-capped rough-shaven old geezer, burned-out by Nazi labour camps, cold English winters and too many cigarettes. He shamed me in front of my friends with his Pidgin English; on one memorable occasion he referred to Mother's Pride bread as 'mummy's brother'. His last fifteen years were to be spent lying, covered in unwashed blankets, on sofas of varying decrepitude. The TV packed in sometime in 1971, halfway through that week's episode of *It's A Knockout*. We couldn't afford to have it repaired and I gave up on the goggle box, never to return.

A curiously Tardis-like spatial dislocation occurred when you walked through our house or any of the others on our side of the street. It was always a surprise to discover that the sizable back gardens were about ten feet lower than the street outside the front door. This area of unexpectedly low land was doubled by taking into account the gardens of the houses backing onto ours – those in Woodlands Avenue. Our own back garden was reached by wooden steps descending from a glass-roofed veranda tacked onto the rear of the house like an after-thought. From the bottom of the steps the land continued to descend several feet towards the once-creosoted fence at the end of the garden.

It was a weedy and spidery zone, the bottom of our garden. The fence was shoed with bricks and these served as anchors for the conical webs of black tunnel spiders, one of whom I named Al Capone and fed regularly with red and black ants, woodlice and earwigs. There was also a chipped bird table in which – during a period I spent playing at being a 'chemist' – I had mixed mud, paint, urine and the odd unfortunate beetle for purposes of experimentation. By 1970 chemistry had been superseded by archaeology. Taking the rusted spade from our basement I set to, working down into the soil and clay at the bottom of the garden. I hoped to find some shards of Roman pottery but instead, after about eighteen inches, I hit the curved surface of a concrete pipe. Casting my spade aside in disgust I immediately gave up on archaeology and moved on to the biological sciences. I converted the cellar into a laboratory by collecting jars of all sorts – jam, pickled onion, potted meat – from around the house and laying them out in ranks on a vast old kitchen table. My favourites were the old 1950s Kilner jars left behind by my mother. Filled with water tinted with colours from my paint box, these provided me with the preservatives, reagents and other chemicals I needed. One day I found a dead blackbird by the old stone bench hidden behind some apple saplings planted by my dad in 1968. I snipped the bird's head off with scissors, laying the dead creature – and his head – on a slate on which I inscribed, using a piece of chalk plucked from the garden's soil, the words: 'A victim of bird disease'.

Had I been a little clearer in my thinking I would've spotted a connection between the concrete pipe at the bottom of my garden and the one in the acre of land where I safely bunked school. Years later I worked out that my garden pipe carried a small watercourse downhill to where it joined the stronger stream that fed through 'the sewer'. Our back garden rested in a river gully.

The Borough of Finchley possessed a still larger river, the Dollis Brook, which ran north to south on the far side of the main road. An alley led between shops and over the railway to where an old lodge house marked the beginning of the path to the brook. The way down to the valley bottom passed between spacious suburban houses. A streamlet ran alongside, on the bank of which grew numerous horse chestnut trees, nettles and – in May – white broad-leaved flowers that smelled of garlic. The path reached the brook just by a golf course and crossed over to the opposite bank via a wooden bridge. In about 1965 a silver, rust-proof structure was erected next to the bridge to carry an ancillary pipeline across the brook. It is still there today – and still free of rust; I continue to refer to it as I did when it first appeared, as 'the new bridge'.

When I was free and relatively unburdened – I mean in the 1960s, before my mother left – I would go down to the brook with my sister and two brothers and we would walk what seemed like miles along the watercourse in either direction. If we turned right at the bridge a causeway with swampy ground to either side would lead us through to civilised parklands complete with swings, lavatories and mowed grass. Left would take us along by the golf course and through miserable twisted trees to a small lake in which we caught sticklebacks and newts. Further on, the tube railway's Mill Hill East branch crossed the river valley on a vast brick viaduct that suddenly came into view high above the dense riverside woodland. Beyond that – having crossed beneath a winding lane busy with traffic – the stream headed through unexplored parkland towards places as yet still unimagined.

Once in that awful winter of 1970 I risked the police and the greenies and revisited the brook. It had probably been two years since I had last been there and the journey from age nine to eleven had carried me through some developmental node-point in which unhappiness had increased enormously. Gone were the sunlit vales of my childhood, replaced by dread: dread in the face of the bullying and poverty; dread in the face of the dismal world with its black arterial roads, damp houses, demands of education and gymnasium.

I resolved on that occasion to follow the brook as far south as I could, intent as I was on unpicking the seam of my imprinted world. Whether I was looking for another land – somewhere happier and safer – or merely responding to some early hint of my interest in topography I don't know. For the first time I journeyed beyond the viaduct, over the busy road and into parklands that clearly belonged to a different world to the one I knew.

It was a land inhabited for the most part by pram-pushing, ringlet-haired mothers who bore, in their slender dark-faced beauty and their fine clothes, a certainty and security alien to me. Their curly-haired and chubby-cheeked children stared at me reprovingly through dark piercing eyes. They had clearly been born into a world that nourished and accepted them gladly, and they instinctively recognised that I was something other. Even the spoilt and well-brushed little lapdogs that ran about on the broad swathe of mown grass before stopping and eyeing me disdainfully seemed to bear an authority in their presence that was denied to me. The houses visible beyond the treelined footpath grew bigger as I marched south. Brightly polished cars clustered around blocks of luxury flats of recent design fitted with big windows revealing pull-down blinds and smart interiors.

Then everything changed suddenly. The walk ended where a major road – at the time I assumed it was the North Circular, though, in fact, it was the Great North Way link between the A406 and the A41 – crossed the brook just by a large lake. As I gazed into the sun-starved riverbed beneath the road bridge, I knew I had reached the far edge of any world I had ever imagined. The undulating silt, filamentous waterweed and rusted detritus resting on the streambed spoke of endings. This place of dumped paint-cans, hubcaps and bike frames uttered one word only: *Terminus*.

2

SCARP'S BEGINNINGS

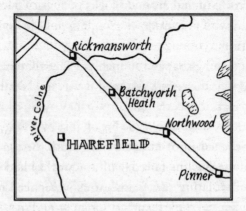

A GLORIOUSLY WEATHERWORN 1962 *BARTHOLOMEW'S Reference Atlas of Greater London*, 'covering the whole of the Metropolitan Police area from Windsor to Tilbury, St Albans to Reigate' has been my constant companion on the walks I've taken over the past twenty years. This item – picked out of a skip behind a charity shop in Camden Town – tells the tale of London and its outliers, large parts of which have now vanished to make way for motorways, regional shopping centres and sports and leisure complexes. The borax works and oil and cake mills that once lined whole stretches of the Thames on its south bank have since been flattened to clear space for supermarkets and high-density housing, as have the proof butts, powder magazines and picquet stables that adorned our military facilities. Of particular interest to me are the clusters of blue circles and rectangles representing the settling tanks and sediment lagoons of myriad sewage farms serving the urban and rural district councils of Hertfordshire and Middlesex. These gland-like node-points of the city disappeared with the coming of countywide main drainage systems in the 1930s and '40s, terminating at Mogden and Deephams Farm in Middlesex and Maple Cross and Rye Meads in Hertfordshire.

Sewage systems are always aligned with (and are occasionally incorporated into) naturally occurring stream flows and their location therefore tells us much about the lay of the land, its physical structure and topology. The Maple Cross purification works, built by the Hertfordshire County Council in the 1950s in order to process sewage flowing from the south Chilterns and the northern face of Scarp, lies deep down in the valley of the river Colne south-west of Rickmansworth. To the north and west of the works the wooded foothills of the Chilterns rear up before dropping again further west towards the Misbourne stream. On the east bank of the river Colne, a broad area of cultivated upland scattered with woods, farms and pockets of housing ascends steeply out of the valley. Perched upon the west edge of this plateau lies the straggling village of Harefield. Further to the north is the sprawling Mount Vernon Hospital. It is this landmass that forms the bulbous western end of Scarp.

I was troubled as to how best to approach the Harefield uplands. I wanted to gain a sense of Scarp's beginnings, to experience through my eyes and the uphill motion of my legs the exact moment when Scarp comes into being. The problem was that the plateau extends for about four miles north to south and would have to be tackled from several different directions if I wanted to gain an understanding of its structure and the relationship between its component parts. In order to do this I decided to undertake a series of walks spread over a fortnight in the summer of 2011.

The first walk – and this was probably the most obvious choice of approach – was directly northwards along the Grand Junction Canal from Uxbridge, a route that closely parallels the river Colne. My hope was that as I headed north I would be presented with a growing sense of Scarp's emergence out of the lower lands to the south. However, I soon discovered that the canal provides little in the way of the broader view due to the dense herbage growing along its edge, which effectively shuts off the walker from the surrounding land. True, I saw chains of lakes tucked between the canal and river and glimpses of the New Denham township – a place I have yet to visit – through gaps in the trees to the west. The A40 Western Avenue linking London to Denham crosses the canal at one point and the drama of the road – its concrete and steel horizontals and verticals and its jarring mix of motion and stability – breaks the tedium somewhat. Some years back I became lost when I strayed from the canal close to the A40. After wandering about in

a thicket of willows and alders I stumbled across a wasteland of derelict factories. The chipped cement floors and
concrete tracks – all that remained after the factory buildings had been demolished – were pierced by fountains of
Canadian fleabane and orange-tinged weld. Everywhere,
scattered amidst the rampant sycamores there were burnt
cars and motor scooters, coils of wiring, its insulation blackened. Masses of Michaelmas daisy showed off their mauve
florets, it being late summer, and buddleias dangled over the
top of every wall left standing, their purple spikes turning to
brown as the hot day phased into a purple night. I have never
been able to find the place again.

It was a hot day and eventually I collapsed, as much from
frustration as exhaustion, next to a gravel extractor rusting
away in a field of buttercups and slept for an hour. On waking
I drank some water and then looked around me: there was the
busy A40 still droning away behind the trees; on the opposite
bank of the canal I could see some luxury flats and a small boy
in a striped T-shirt riding a bicycle. A brightly painted house-
boat chugged past on the canal, its young passengers waving
merrily to me and me waving back with less enthusiasm. Of
Scarp, though, I could see nothing.

I headed further north with diminishing expectations and
eventually found what I was looking for, though the impact
was less dramatic than I had hoped it would be. Scarp first
appears – at least in summer – as a swathe of distant full-
leafed trees billowing some distance beyond the rooftops of
an emergent new suburb (possibly built on the site of my lost

factory complex) by a large and languid boat-packed marina. That day – after I walked a few more yards – it disappeared again as the canal-side flora once more edged in close to the water.

It took another mile or two of avoiding towpath cyclists before I finally got what I wanted. After walking beneath the Moor Hall road bridge I noticed that the vegetation on the canal's opposite bank had thinned out and the land on its far side was sloping steeply upwards to some large houses on the edge of what my map told me was Harefield village. My excitement grew as my eyes followed a hawthorn hedge on its half-mile journey uphill between two fields before it terminated in a clump of oaks. Suddenly I was overwhelmed by a sense of standing on the edge of something improbably grand, of staring up at the emergence of a solid and tangible presence. The next step was to get up there.

I came to a bridge and crossed the canal, walking upwards onto the broad plateau along a hollow way flanked by pleached hedges. At one point I stopped to look back across the Colne Valley towards the Chilterns and if I had ever harboured doubts concerning Scarp's existence, the view I gained banished them instantly. The broad patchwork of fields woven onto the slopes of the plateau dropped vertiginously to black wedges of woodland far below. Through the trees I caught glimpses of lakes sparkling in the afternoon sun. I was suspended on the very lip of the land.

Of far greater interest was a walk I took four days later to the east of, but parallel with, the canal. This ran along the back of a chain of three low hills that dangle southwards off Scarp's western head, linking Bayhurst Wood, a nub of wooded high ground on the south face of Scarp, with the outskirts of Uxbridge. I felt that walking these hills – which appear on several of my older contour maps as small brown globules – would serve as a sort of prelude prior to the main event. For the sake of this account I have numbered them from south to north Hills One, Two and Three.

Once again I started out from Uxbridge town centre. As I walked along Harefield Road and then gently uphill through dead-quiet residential streets I felt a sense of anticipation, as if I was zoning in on the first murmurings of a forgotten legend or the hermetic tail end of what was once common knowledge, now woven into the fabric of the landscape. Finally I broke free of the cloying mass of houses onto Hill One, which is crowned by the treelined and grassy expanse of Uxbridge Common. I struck diagonally ahead across the grass and felt a surge of triumph as I looked eastwards down through a sports field and blocks of woodland onto south Middlesex. To the north, further along my chosen route, a tall battlemented brick watertower built in 1900 for the Rickmansworth and Uxbridge Valley Water Company rose over the rooftops of the houses on the edge of the common and pointed the way ahead.

After passing the tower I came to where the A40 cuts dramatically through the gap between Hills One and Two at Swakeleys Roundabout. I spent a moment watching the traffic flowing west, a vague unease rising in me at the sight of thick storm clouds building somewhere far off. I crossed over and then left the road leading directly to Harefield, slipping onto a side street to the left called The Drive. This led through a discreet and opulent suburb of large attractive residences, each distinct in design, each set firmly in its own grounds. The thin brown contour lines marked on the OS map I used that day indicated that there was a steep drop down to the canal and river from behind the houses on the left and I wondered at how I had no sense of this, at how shut off I was from the land's shape as I walked between the green pantiled bungalows, pseudo-Tudor villas, the defoliated gardens packed with highly polished cars and fitted with spiked electric gates.

The trees growing by the road – cypresses, sequoias and scotch pines – were clearly residues of a sizable estate that the suburb had been built over. In fact, The Drive was at one time the driveway serving pilastered and stuccoed Harefield Place, which I came across a little further along. Built in 1786 for Sir Roger Newdigate, Harefield Place later served as a hospital for the Middlesex County Council but is now the headquarters of Blockbusters, the video hire company. I was a bit put out finding something as banal as a corporate head office on what felt like a holy pilgrimage. The suited and bespectacled executive type who approached me in the car park and asked me if I needed help meant no harm but I wasn't feeling very communicative and, after muttering that I was merely taking a look around, I crouched down by the laurels and consulted my maps, the quicker to leave the place.

I soon hit a track heading downhill in a north-westerly direction and followed this, the drop of the land to the right granting views across the valley of the river Pin to the wooded expanse of Scarp two miles to the north.

I passed a little row of cottages and entered Uxbridge Golf Course (the first of many such encountered on Scarp), its green spattered with the white stars of lesser stitchwort, and after walking a few yards downhill, crossed a stile onto a track on the right which led me across a field back to the grass-verged road to Harefield, which I had left earlier.

I had no option now but to follow the road northwards, dangerous though it was. Cars, horse-trailers and a surprising number of trucks swept rapidly along the road in both directions and I had to use my eyes and ears fully in order to keep track of what was happening around me. This became particularly crucial as I descended the northern edge of Hill Two to where a bridge bore the road across a dead-straight stretch of the Denham Railway, which passed deep below in a cutting. The grass verges faded and dense belts of hawthorn pressed close to the road as it approached a sharp curve. With nowhere to run in the event of a vehicle suddenly appearing before me I had to rely solely on my ears to stay safe. A small roadside shrine consisting of scattered flowers and a rude wooden cross inscribed with the name Michael did nothing to reassure me.

Off to the left, just before the railway, a concrete service road ran down to a sizable scrapyard tucked up against the railway tracks and numerous lorries laden with rusting metal rattled and hissed past me before turning down the track. Despite my worries at being flattened by a 4×4 or a truck, a sense of excitement rose ever strongly in me as I closed on my quarry. Later I passed Highways House Farm on the right with its spectacular seventeenth-century barn. Here, between Hills Two and Three, the land flattened out on the left onto the river plain. It was a scruggy, gravelly, rabbit-infested place packed with unwelcoming forests of creeping thistle. Pylons seemingly strutted across the acidic meadows and always there was the sound of cars, cars, cars streaking up and down the lanes.

I cut across the south-east corner of Hill Three, which rises to Braemar Farm before dropping down to New Years Green Lane. Close to the farm there is a tall mound of smashed concrete that a farmhand told me was part of the remains of the old Wembley Stadium. I dumped my rucksack and clambered to the top of the pile. Facing to the south-east and turning clockwise in a circle on my informal ferro-concrete plinth, I saw the following cardinal points arrayed on the larger dial of the surrounding country: the tower blocks of the Dragon Estate in Brentford (ten miles distant); Uxbridge, with its major building works, its vast multi-storeyed car parks (three miles); Heathrow Airport's Terminal 5 (eight miles), Queen Anne's Hill in Chertsey (twelve miles); St George's Hill (south of Weybridge in Surrey – fifteen miles); Crab Hill (an Iron-Age fort near Gerrards Cross in Bucks – four miles); Breakspear House in Harefield (not even a mile); Mount Vernon Hospital and Moor Park, both on Scarp (two miles); the Belmont Mound, near Stanmore (six miles);

Premier House (a tall modernist office block in Station Road, Edgware – seven miles); the green-roofed National Institute for Medical Research in Mill Hill (nine miles) and the grey smear of Hampstead Heath (twelve miles).

Across New Years Green Lane a track climbs what could be taken as the edge of Scarp proper towards Bayhurst Wood, with its mix of well-spaced sessile and pedunculate oak, tall grey beech trees and coppiced hornbeam. Between the wood and Harefield lies a broad band of flat barren heath land infested in late summer with purple flowered hardheads and broad-leaved burdock. Cutting through its centre, north to south, runs a stream (buried here but traceable through periodically spaced ductile plates mounted on concrete cylinders) that rises by Mount Vernon Hospital. Further downstream the waters finally surface, feeding a sizable ornamental pond in the yard of Highways House Farm, passed earlier.

A particularly strident line of pylons follows the stream's course and adds a peculiar intensity to the landscape: this is definitely a place of history and power, one of those Celtic 'thin places', where a sense of something other lurks just behind the visible. At one time, a few years back there were nettle-edged ponds, but they seem to have dried out. I love to sit by the track crossing below the high-tension cables and imagine that I'm somewhere in the Ukraine, circa 1952, staring up at these triumphant monuments to the electrification of my region. I'm a veterinary surgeon working on a *sovhoz* located somewhere unpronounceable deep in the shimmering wheat plains. I see tractors and fat sows; I see Olga, the pig-tailed farm nurse who comes to me at night. In the evening I smoke cheap cigarettes and drink vodka. I will die of cancer in 1972. Proximity flight: that's what I call this using of environment to trigger mental journeys to another place and time in which the same stimuli can be found. I find it lifts my sense of the environment out of its codified framework and into fresh possibilities of interpretation, my eyes wiped clean by the resultant defamiliarisation or – in keeping with my Soviet theme – *ostranenie*, a term first used by the Russian theorist Viktor Shklovsky in 1925.

Ahead, the footpath cuts across fields maddened with dyer's rocket, spear plume thistle and Oxford ragwort, the ground broken by broad white bald patches where the chalk underlying the district comes to the surface. It then drops down into an area of low lying and fetid woodland addled with duckweed-coated ponds. This leads directly through to Harefield Church with its old gravestones and its well-known ANZAC cemetery. From here a road runs a mile uphill to Harefield.

My final walk began at Rickmansworth, on the north bank of the Colne. A quick stagger west took me down the small market town's narrow high street to a large roundabout from which radiated roads to the Chalfonts, Northwood and Denham. I followed the last of these through the drab suburb of Money Hill before turning onto a quiet road on the left – Drayton's Ford Lane – which led down to a narrow bridge crossing a side-stream running alongside the Colne. At one time this minor waterway marked the boundary between Middlesex and Hertfordshire.

As I followed the lane, a lake appeared on the left beyond which I could see a cliff-face studded with nodules of chalk. This was clearly one of the numerous gravel and chalk quarries which at one time gave Harefield an almost industrial air.

Through, through, I walked through to a bewildering tangle of canal, river, hatch and ditch; to a madness of twitchers and cyclists, derelict industries hidden in arboreal swamp and always, just beyond the trees, a sense of rising land, of Scarp's face staring down at me. The whole of the Colne Valley is a naturalist's heaven and remains curiously overlooked by the London crowd. There are also the inevitable lakes on which numerous islands – some floating – have been built by conservation volunteers, providing sanctuary for birds. Reading an informational plaque I noted that the Moschatel (*Adoxa moschatellina*) grows around Stocker's Lake, a particularly broad body of water. This is a plant I have often read of (mainly in old Victorian and Edwardian floras where it is usually described as Town Hall Clock on account of the clock-like form of its green flowers) but have never seen. Unfortunately, the day I discovered this was at the end of June and Moschatel flowers in April, so I had missed it.

I got lost in a maze of midge-infested footpaths and eventually surfaced by the Grand Junction Canal at Stocker's House, a rather stern brick building which towers over the canal lock. Behind it stands an old brick and wooden-beamed farmhouse (Stocker's Farm) and several misshapen barns. However, it was the fields sloping down to the canal that interested me the most. I was on the northern tip of Scarp's western extremity.

A footpath runs from Stocker's House up into the hills, initially following a shallow gulley down which a small stream named the Springwell trickles. At one time it was known as the Gulch Well. The botanist, John Blackstone, who spent the years 1734–35 studying the flora of Harefield during a protracted stay with his parents-in-law, the Ashbys at Breakspear House, described it thus in his *Fasciculus Plantarum circa Harefield* (1737):

> 'This place is particularly fine on the account of an extraordinarily fine spring call'd Gulch-well that arises at the foot of a chalk hill and produces at its first appearance, with a very strong current a body of water two feet deep and four feet broad.'

On the day I visited the stream was nowhere near as deep or broad as Blackstone described.

Douglas Kent's *Historical Flora of Middlesex* (1975), a compilation and update of all previous Middlesex floras (including Trimen and Dyer's excellent *Flora of Middlesex* of 1869, itself a compilation of many earlier floras) mentions the Springwell with great frequency, perhaps because the closeness of the chalk to the surface in the area gives rise to several species of calcicolous plant rare elsewhere in Middlesex. Among those mentioned is the *Blackstonia perfoliata* or Yellow-wort, named in honour of John Blackstone by William Hudson in his *Flora*

Anglica of 1762. Yellow-wort, a species of gentian, was unfortunately rendered extinct in Middlesex by chalk quarrying during the 1960s.

The path leads upwards along the Springwell to Cooks Wood, the entrance to which is another segment of the boundary between Middlesex and Hertfordshire, marked here by a coal tariff post. It then strikes off further uphill onto a broad convex meadow with views northwards over Money Hill into the foothills of the Chilterns.

On the day I visited the field was smothered with the yellow flowers of Lady's bedstraw, an Elizabethan strewing herb that smells of fresh hay when dried. As I stood there, eating the cheese and tomato sandwich I'd picked up earlier in Rickmansworth, I could sense my mind feeling its way around the area, trying to grasp the configurations of the downs and draw them into the cortex so I could carry the Harefield district with me wherever I went.

The track eventually hits Springwell Lane, the road to Hill End and Harefield, at Cripps House Farm. There is something depressing about Hill End with its modern houses, its concretised front gardens, its rectitude, and I passed through rapidly.

For the third time in a fortnight I approached Harefield with its old pubs, and its sculpturesque village sign depicting a leaping hare and a map of Australia. Passing a chemist where I'd bought some opiated cough mixture several years previously, I turned right, off the main street and, following an alleyway that ran beside a group of modern flats, I came out onto the edge of the plateau overlooking the Colne, far below. I settled down on

a bench by a footpath designated as part of the Hillingdon Trail
and wrote up my notes. As evening closed in, orange street lights
began to flicker far off on the hills opposite. A blackbird chuck-
led somewhere close by and I felt myself merge with the deep
peacefulness of the mauve woodlands and the mumbling of the
distant M25. I found myself thinking of all the roads I'd walked,
all the corners turned, rotted fence posts passed in my search
for the essence of Harefield. Once more I saw the geostation-
ary hoverflies, smashed wash basins and fly-tipped sofas I'd met
on my journeys. And all around me, as I passed from sweating
exhaustion into relaxation and then surrender, Harefield became
a limpid globe of light as Scarp absorbed me into its first station.

*

There is a mythic meeting of powerlines at infinity, the high-
tension cables slung towards Denham fading to spiders' webs
hanging in rafters, to the cooling ivy that wraps itself around
me. I walk the lane past Breakspear, Mr Ashby's fine resi-
dence, and climb onto the rusticated retaining wall holding
the twisted trees from the road, the better to survey the workings. Everywhere there are cement mixers, scaffoldings and
UV-jacketed whistling Jack Smiths. The persistent thrum of a
generator somewhere on the other side of the caravanserai of
works offices sounds over the outhouses and the lodge house.

Breakspear is being broken into separate living spaces, all way
beyond my pocket. A riding instructor jiggles her jodhpured
buttocks down by the composting shed but it is the Tudor dovecote

that draws me and as I recover from the rigours of my climb out
of the valley I feel myself passing into its brick walls and upwards
through the timbered cupola to its ornate and timeless clock face.
Circling, minute by minute, I am dialled through on–off heat,
cold, light, dark, rain and sleet, watching a movement from panta-
loons and merkins through to these luxury flats and slug-like cars.

Slip, Motorway, round my ankles if you must; drag me into
your petroleum future. You will pass too, ending crotcheted
by red leaves of herb Robert, stars of cow thistle. I see your
car crashes. I see economies collapse. I sense the unspoken
family secrets; I see the white cow-gate lit by sunshine. I am
the centre. I am buttressed stone walls. I am oak rafters and the
soft flap of doves' wings in cool corners. See the de Havilland
Mosquito push overhead, Hatfield bound. See sweet Brian
Connolly sitting and playing guitar in the meadow. He's out
of his rocket on mushrooms, his hair as fair as hay. Now his
face grows furrowed and worn as he ages into knock-knees and
long-johns. Now his corpse is laid out and still I stand. See my
thrust through time, my doves flown high in circles over tall
oaks I knew as saplings. I am the pivot around which it swings,
the spigot through which it all flows. I push down to worm-
holes and into the moist darkness beneath your bullied present
day. Now there are Kindles, now you are wired to Androids.
Now there is a white flash and everything is swept away.

I shrivel and die, passing into stumpy, pock-faced John
Blackstone, apothecary and herbalist, in his two summers
spent at Breakspear with the Ashby family. I smell the stink of
the piggery and hear the simmering birds early in the day. All

the heights are an open palm – God's very handiwork apparent
in the forms of the world around me. March brings the yellow
flowered, heart-leaved pilewort, the roots ground into animal
fat and applied as a paste to the hanging nodules, the pained
tush. In April I walk tracks still muddy to Ruislip Common
where I find the checquer'd daffodil growing in Maud Fields,
as reported by Mr Ashby these last forty years. Their petals
are pointed at the tip and there is a nodding grace in their
beauty. The country people call them snakes' heads. Later I
rage in haylofts and froth in the heat, or sleep with the cattle,
my face pressed close to sweet-smelling sainfoin. There are
black-tongued ravings as the devil's guts winds its madness of
tendrils about our garden endeavour, my loneliness coagulating on the hot flagstones by the buttery. Everything stares back
at me as I peer out through rheumy eyes. I'm overdressed, my
frockcoat stiff with dried sweat, my periwig a fine home for
fleas and lice.

I sketch the sundews growing in the boggy soil behind the
family house and the Elms (which I recorded first in this county
of Middlesex), their tufted flowers crimson like the feathers
of the cockatoo. I'm happy here, free of London's dirt, and
write at night to my friend Sir Hans Sloane. I curse the Royal
Surveyor, James King, after catching him spying on me from
behind the pumping station at Drayton's Ford. Mr King, with
his political arithmetic, seeks to tabulate, correlate and fabri-
cate everything, distilling Harefield down to charts and tables
for the glory of money not God.

Trickle away, Sir Soil; slave, young Master Ant; uncoil,

Mademoiselle Fern. Fungus opens like the newfangled umbrella. If there be a God then this surely is as much his work as our fine fleets or the jowled and brandied ministers who govern. There is a smouldering heath fire across the valley and bees high in the yews; they dart up and down, up and down in a madness, gold as ambers brought from Courland as I splutter, washing my face with my silk kerchief by the gulch. The Quakers – those hard-working plain folk – stare at me and tap their temples as ripe after ale I sleep among the stooks. I wake in the cooling evening and head off alone, wanting nobody, feeling nobody. Later, I note the rare Bay-leaved willow near Mr Ashby's brick kiln.

What wonder informs these new natural sciences! What craziness interweaves with the discrete entities, throwing its fullness of crafted detail into the pavanne of evening midges, their cloudy romances grey ghosts by the towpath. I pass the thumping copper mill, hellish behind the copse down by the river. It nestles, a dark energy of labour in its correct place before fading to restaurants, production companies and gymnasiums, the sweet sweaty scent of skunk drifting across the gated car parks. And this whole land, these two springs and summers, is the heart of the kingdom of a God on Earth!

I surface towards evening, the silhouettes of poplars pointing upwards towards an early star. A helicopter churns the soured air and tilts towards Northolt while a wasp-faced electric train slices through to the brick bridge spanning the county border. Here, where grass and nettle give over to barren dry dust; in this dead land between pink-sailed leisure boating and ferocious women on barges; here, where a first fag was smoked in 1952 and the distraught madman wanted in connection with a murder hid out in a derelict rutting shed – here I halt and unroll the sleeping bag.

3

MOOR PARK

THE FLAT-ROOFED AND MODERNIST branch of Waitrose, sited on the upper level of Rickmansworth Underground Station's brown-brick multi-storey car park, has large south-facing plate-glass windows that look out over the rooftops of Rickmansworth town and across the Colne Valley. Pop in under the guise of buying some granary bread or baked beans and take the time to stare out on the view. To the right, slanting upwards and away to the north-west, are the Harefield uplands. Directly ahead and barely visible through a gap in the houses on the opposite slope of the valley is a flash of high ground punctured by tiny crescents of white indicating the presence of sand bunkers. It is Batchworth Golf Course, on the north edge of Batchworth Heath.

Further eastwards, there is yet another bulge of land, this resembling an elevated arboretum, so prevalent are the silhouettes – distinctive, even, from this distance – of exotic pines, maples and spectacularly broad-girthed oaks outlined against the sky. You are gazing at Moor Park, site of one of the most exclusive golf clubs in Hertfordshire. (Another prospect of Moor Park – this from the upper levels of the Gade Car Park, just off Watford High Street, some miles to the north-east – places it more firmly within the overall structure of Scarp. Moor Park clearly forms a link connecting Harefield and Batchworth Heath with the slopes of Oxhey Wood and the extensive ridge of land taking in Harrow Weald Common and Stanmore.)

A walk south from Rickmansworth Station, crossing the high street and the town ditch (where, in 1999 during a solo ecological survey I found a fine specimen freshwater shrimp *Gammarus pulex,* and then promptly fell in) leads to an austere road bridge spanning the Colne and canal and on into the new suburb of Batchworth. From here, a stepped ramp between two houses on Sherfield Avenue pushes through the unkempt eco-margin of the Batchworth Golf Course on to Juniper Hill. There is a sense of displacement there, amidst the belts of furze, the expensively equipped golfers and the brightly coloured metal flags marking the holes. As the breeze blows in from the surrounding countryside a feeling is attained of having escaped from the heavy gravity of the endless and unnameable townships and colonies smeared about the outer reaches of London.

A track runs along the west edge of the course, hugging the upper contour lines before dropping down across a narrow valley at the bottom of which a mass of dock weeds suggests the presence of a subsurface stream. The track comes out onto a busy road which climbs from Rickmansworth over Woodcock Hill towards Harefield. The walk uphill leads to a footpath on the left. This crosses an area of remote countryside to London Road, which connects Rickmansworth with Northwood. Follow this road to the right as it ascends Batchworth Heath Hill to a busy road junction. On the left, a short distance down the road to Northwood and Pinner, there is the entrance to a path, its length lined with old oaks, which follows the old Hertfordshire and Middlesex boundary for two miles, dropping into a wooded valley overlooked by pylons before crossing a succession of silent streets. Passing between the ends of large back gardens, the path crosses the Metropolitan Line by a footbridge and eventually reaches Potters Hill, where walks downhill lead to either Northwood or Pinner, depending on which route is taken.

As cars circle the roundabout at Batchworth Heath Hill, before striking out for Northwood, Harefield or Rickmansworth, look eastwards along a short road that disappears through a gap in the trees. Hidden back behind the treeline there stands a majestic Doric archway flanked by lodge houses. It is the main entrance to the Moor Park estate and golf course.

Moor Park is the name given to both the parkland attached to Moor Park House and the exclusive suburb built on its outer edges during the 1920s and '30s. The estate is essentially an immense mound of London clay topped by sand and gravel. It is currently shared by the Rickmansworth and Moor Park Golf Clubs. The former, owned by Hertsmere Council, is open for public use on a drop-in basis. The Moor Park Club is strictly members only and incorporates the best part of the old park, including the sumptuous Moor Park mansion – which serves as the clubhouse – and the faded remnants of the once-equally impressive Italian gardens laid out in the 1830s.

To enter Moor Park, preferably through the Doric archway, is to slip into what feels like enemy territory. The walk along the winding drive towards the mansion, passing patches of birch, bracken and – in autumn – clusters of fly agarics, always feels in some way to be forbidden. As you repeatedly step onto the roadside verge to avoid the cars passing in either direction, paranoia kicks in. Are those shadowy figures staring out through the car windows looking down on you in disdain?

Years back – probably around September 1998 – I wandered onto Moor Park golf course for the first time as I approached the end of a walk that had begun that morning at Mill Hill, some miles to the east. I still recall the first glimpse I had of the clubhouse and how preposterous I thought it was. Built in the 1720s for Benjamin Styles, a merchant who made a fortune out of the South Sea Bubble, Moor Park House represented everything I resented about privilege and wealth. The gleaming façade of Portland stone; the roof-height portico *prostyle* with its Corinthian pillars; the balustrade running along the building's flat roof: all these signified to me the presence of The Enemy. The large expanse of the car park out front was packed with well-polished vehicles; waistcoated waiting staff stood smoking outside the rusticated orangery attached to the main bulk of the mansion by a gently curving colonnade. Everything about the place spoke of exclusiveness and presumption and I hurried past, certain my ripped walking jeans, my threadbare purple rucksack and my ludicrous gait would draw the attention of whatever passed for security.

In fact, this has never happened in my experience, despite numerous subsequent visits, though some of the golfers seem slightly wary of my shuffling, muttering presence. Repeated exposure to Moor Park over the years since has slowly changed my attitude to the place. Today I see it as a nexus of complex cultural affiliations.

The history of Moor Park is well described in *Moor Park: the Grosvenor Legacy* by Martyn Pedrick (1989), a copy of which was kindly presented to me by the club secretary during the research for this book. I won't bore the reader with a detailed inventory of the various artworks that fill the house as described in Mr Pedrick's work. Much as the club takes great pride in its Paladin clubhouse with its interior wall paintings by James Thornhill and its exquisite wooden staircase, it is the views from certain points on the golf course itself that hold me transfixed and provide me with a sense of being on Scarp. In particular, a curious circular rough known as the Bathend Clump (approximately 120 metres above sea level and reputedly the site of a Bronze-Age encampment), grants a Pisgah prospect of the wooded lower slopes of the Chilterns beyond Watford.

*

Exposure to the mossy pavements, high-hedges and broad-fronted quality villas that skirt the east side of the golf course wakens some port-supping retrograde hidden inside me, a latent Tory who wishes that he too belonged in this discreet conservation zone with its statued gardens and gravel drives. Born in 1936 and established in my profession by the early 1960s, I barely noticed the bell-bottomed hairy Dionysiac of those who were born five or so years later than me, and what little of it did register – a somewhat fey computer engineer who opted out of the city firm I work for in order to study electronic music in Brazil; the ungrateful son of an elder colleague of mine who was caught making LSD in his cottage in Wales – left me wholly contemptuous and proud to be non-comprehending, totally devoted as I was to more socially acceptable modes of intoxication, these provided by the wine merchants and my doctor. I was never young, though I have surpassed myself in growing old and – if I say so myself – it suits me.

And here is my fine Dutch-style house, with its stained-glass window depicting a windmill and a boy smoking a meerschaum. Here are my neighbours: curly-haired and sensible Mr Bolt on the right, his collection of lovingly polished sports cars parked out front – in some fit of ageing bachelorism he has named his house Nadgers; Mr and Mrs Jitendra Pandya on the left call their house Praan (a Bengali word meaning Stream of Life). They are very polite and always smile when they pass me in the street, though their daughter is angrily third-world militant, even as she clubs all night in town or flies off regularly on the back of the family wealth.

And when I go into the back garden in the evening to smoke by the potting shed, I experience the dark mass of Moor Park rising over the garden fence as a geomantic node-point, a nodule of energy pumping its pure stream of (English) life directly through to me. This owl-haunted tree-tangled giant rears over me as I sit on my daughter's swing under the apple tree and speaks of history and stability, of an England that will never fade. I hear its voice also in the predictable jokes of my fellow club members (for how could I not join up, steep though the cost is?), the rakes down from the Chalfonts in their MG Midgets, hawk-eyed senior policemen and silver-haired barristers with whom they share a shoddy mutualism.

And in the frosty morning, when I guide my PowaKaddy electric golf trolley across the crisp green and the coots slide on the icy pond, I enjoy once more this most civilised of games. I hear the 'puck' of the iron hitting the ball; I luxuriate in my buttock-clenched arch-backed satisfaction, the virile poise maintained surprisingly well in one my age, as away the ball carries before glugging down into an England that persists despite the polyglot entreaties of the more recently signed-up members of the club. After returning to the clubhouse my business affairs are discussed with colleagues in hushed tones out of earshot of all this mess, all this displaced personage. Our condemnation of these somewhat exotic gentlemen is expressed quietly from fear of retaliation and always, on finding another who shares my views on this matter, there is at first the relief of identification and then – inexplicably – the shame.

Back in 1971 I took my brother and his pal the Tory MP Reginald Maudling around the course. Maudling was in a lather about Northern Ireland and the imminent visit of Alice Cooper to our shores. 'Lock 'em up I say' he barked, speaking of the internment without trial he was shortly to implement. Not that this affected his game, you understand. Reggie was renowned for his old-fashioned palm grip, for his sitting well down to the shot and, above all, for the number and ferocity of his waggles. He was equally master of the artistic hook, his right foot creeping ever a little farther back during his waggles till he was poised for the shot. His best that afternoon was when he cut up the pin with a spoon on the 14th hole.

Unfortunately Reggie was pissed in both the American and British senses of the word and the combination was explosive:

'The problem with the *Guardian*,' he roared when I mentioned a recent editorial comment on his policies regarding immigration, 'is that it's written by Central Europeans for Central Africans.'

'Get off the fairway, you bloody fool,' he shouted as some lanky-haired relic of the 'progressive' era nosed along the public footpath, fully cognisant of his right to do so. I secretly agreed with Reggie on this one, wishing these Chelsea-booted student-types, doubtlessly living on Arts Council handouts and wandering around the stockbroker belt with their cameras and notebooks while trying to reduce the lives of people like us to a few unpalatable scraps of avant-garde prose-poetry, would simply sod off.

Yet Reggie wasn't exactly easy to accommodate either. As his oaths sounded across the 13th hole, fading into the trees somewhere in the vicinity of the ornate William and Mary seats on the old North Terrace, I felt myself yearning to escape from this toad-like dipsomaniac and apologist for the god-awful civic architecture springing up like boils in our market towns. Later, probably in no real fit state to drive, he left us, roaring off in his Jag to visit his alma mater at Merchant Taylor School just over the railway line.

After a round I like to visit the lake just by where Capability Brown's Temple of the Wind blew down in a gale in 1936. As I smoke and stare at the temple's surviving pillars, scattered in the grounds of Connell, Ward and Lucas's wondrous ocean liner-like house, reputedly built for an admiral back in 1937, I think of Moor Park's history, its roots dating back to Cardinal Wolsey's palace which once stood down in the valley just behind the clubhouse of our golfing neighbours at Sandy Lodge. I ponder the great days of Lord Ebury, who built the golf course, of sweet Aggie Harwood who broke the club record at the age of seventeen back in 1918 – I see her outlined in her Oxford bags against the lowering sun on the upper course, her brow furrowed as she follows the ball. I think of Bob Hope, over from the States in the late 1980s to watch the tournaments named in his honour. Though never funny in my estimation,

he was, however, superb with the putt, his ragged octogenar-
ian face split by a 'comic' grin at each successful cut. I think of
moustachioed Major-General Robert Urquhart playing a round
in his maroon beret on the eve of Operation Market Garden
before assembling with his fellow planners at the sand table
in an upstairs room at the mansion for a final briefing before
the jump. They linger here, these ghosts, providing continuity
to the place. Sometimes I fancy I see them carrying their golf
bags past the lake or shagging in the roughs as evening settles
in. I hope these apparitions of my over-malted mind will never
leave.

There is another presence here at Moor Park that refuses to
concede its place, this hidden behind the shops at the lower end
of Main Avenue, opposite the station. The derelict and overgrown Murco filling station whispers to me and draws me in
through its screen of wire safety fencing, its thicket of buddleia
every time I pass it. And, I admit, I visit once in a while to
sneak a fag there when my wife becomes particularly roused
by concerns for my health. As I stand amid the ornamental
cypresses, now run wild, the smoke from my Cigaronnes waft-
ing across the 1960s-style pumps, each mounted on a lozenge
of gorgeous blue tiling, I feel my bowels loosen; I take pleasure
in my farts as my body releases its grip on my packed life and
I sense my mind being drawn down into the flaking hypogeum
of the drained petrol tank deep below. Settling in the still-
ness of this echoing unichapel, I feel the whole suburb passing
through me. My thought waves begin to merge with the lives
of those who inhabit these inscrutable streets. It is a rich and

ancient storybook I read from at such moments and if I were to transliterate the contents of its curled yellowing pages, the result would be something akin to the mid-twentieth-century modernist poetry I occasionally indulge in reading (but don't tell my wife about any of this).

As the white delivery van belonging to Tolly & Sons ('Purveyors of the Finest Quality Meats and Poultry') pulls up in the accommodation road behind the parade of shops, I emerge, altered and refreshed, from my reconnection to the tap-root. And I surprise myself with this experience, each time I go through it, returning afterwards to my library and settling down into a sort of immersion, a melding with the moist leaf-fall, the unnameable fungi of my autumnal mind, only to deny it later when the practical difficulties of my life regain their hold on me.

Eventually I end up at the Murco again and once more experience that thrill; a sense of stepping into a broader framework, one that paradoxically reduces me to a component of the scene while at the same time it elevates me towards a truer, richer sense of the suburb's inner will. And I am the king of the stockbroker belt. And all of Moor Park resides inside me. As the fine late autumn mizzle hangs over the approach roads I hit the underlying circuitry, the pulse-energy that pushes up to manifest as parked cars and ornate garden gates; I see illicit encounters in fitted bedrooms, experience epiphanies in octagonal gazebos, by stone rollers. I stare out of any window any time these last eighty years. I kiss every belly, stroke every thigh. I pass into attics and through packed tea chests, savouring the scent of musty old newspapers – 1925, 1957, 1971 – wedged tightly around rose-patterned china dinner sets, framed photographs of dogs long dead, useless Christmas trinkets, unmarked calendars of winter scenes or sports cars. And the entire suburb is a groove sensation, a humming colony lit deep in ancient woodland. It is igniting, burning, its flames throwing their lurid light upwards through my whisky-shot eyes onto the ivory of my wife's fine-boned face as she lowers herself on me.

Later, I wander down Moor Lane, weaving through the brackens on the edge of the dip down to the river's sump. These are flat chittering wastes set in low-lying darkness born of the coming together of the rivers Gade and Colne. Finally, a smoking chimney appears up ahead and I visit Gregory at Offa House, supping Blue Mountain coffee and whisky in his panelled study. We talk of the Mercian King while the rooftops of the houses opposite, on their raised side road built onto the slope of the golf course, seem to rise and then fall, rise and then fall again, before tumbling to brick dust and scorched strewn relics, to the stink of ashes washed away by black rain. A child's arm pokes from mounds of stone. An ornate hand mirror lies smashed in the waste. A feral cat whips away through brambles into the darkness.

And all the tendrileferous streets and alleys are walked in one winter's night, my coat's collar raised, my notebooks later stored in lacquered boxes. I think of Tolpits Lane – built by Cardinal Wolsey to connect his palace with Watford Town – as it winds through to Camelot head offices and derelict railway lines. I think of the withy meadows down in the valley, the bricked-up pillbox waiting under pylons and the hissing trains crawling along the viaduct. I am frog-spawn in limpid pools and gull's eyes watching from overhead. I am newt mouth and fly scrawl. I die on sun-drenched white walls of industrial estates each autumn, fading into the deeper mind, the all-seeing leaf-faced Mumbler down by the shire ditch where the river winds past the pumping station with its iron bolts as big as fists. These angles and facets are jewels in a quarry of stone. Their dreams float on the river and gurgle into dark. They pound and oscillate among the dials and megawatts of the Watford powerhouse and spread out along the rivers Gade and Chess, passing through chalk caves, caravan parks and industry.

As I wandered off at dusk, following the course of the railway south, I passed shadowy groups of commuters making their way home for dinner. Tracing further along the road towards an electricity substation hidden in the overgrowth by a culverted brook, I looked back over my shoulder at a tumble-haired and freckled woman who smiled at me before crossing the road and away. As she disappeared down a side street I felt I carried inside me a gift. So often this probing is rewarded. So often something is delivered up.

A damp and cold Sunday night in November 1975 and I stood on the pavement outside my home in Woodside Park Road, North Finchley and watched the flame-animated shadows of the trees writhing across the gardens and the parked cars like the dancing limbs of black Kali, goddess of destruction. As serious-faced firemen began pulling red canvas hoses from a drum mounted on the rear of their tender, a scattering of sparks rose into sight above the orange glow of the fire eating its way into the back of my neighbour's house. A loud pop, probably caused by a window breaking in the heat, brought new urgency to the firemen's efforts. As I listened to their yells and saw the fear in the faces of the onlookers standing in clumps across the road, I knew that the life I had lived to date was ending; shortly I would be moving on. That night, as I lay in bed, I realised that I was going to have to pay the price for what I'd done. I woke up in the morning sick and unable to believe my resolution.

It was the day I started – and ended – my first-ever job, as a warehouse boy at a pet-food manufactory nearby. My old man worked there and he'd had a word with the management on my behalf. Not that I was grateful: I didn't want to work in a warehouse, I felt it was nowhere near good enough for me, and anyway, I was nervous of my new workmates with their bad teeth, their weathered and weary faces. No sooner had I arrived than I'd made my mind up to leave. All morning I shifted heavy boxes of pet food, placing them on the ceiling-high metal racks to await collection. Lunchtime arrived and I wandered off, never to return.

I walked up the Great North Road to the 1950s police station at the top of Friern Barnet Lane and climbed the reinforced-concrete steps to the glass-panelled double-doors at the entrance. As I passed through this well-lit vestibule of post-war rationality I knew that I was entering new lands, that the vague yet powerful imperatives that drove me were about to strip me to my bare essentials as effectively as any Hindi deity. I approached a bored-looking desk sergeant and told him the purpose of my visit. Flustered, he asked me to sit down and went to get assistance. Moments later I looked up to see a tall slim man dressed in smart jeans and a T-shirt standing there looking at me intensely. I nodded to him and he stepped forward, leaned over towards me, and spoke quietly into my ear.

'Nicky, is it?'

'Yes.'

'Hello, I'm Detective Constable Whitely. So you've set fire to your neighbour's house, you say?'

'Yes. And my school. Twice.'

Eyebrows were raised; the desk sergeant smirked.

'I see. And why did you do that?'

'Dunno. I felt confused.'

'Are you aware of what you're telling me?'

'Yes. I just want to give myself up.'

'Here, come with me Nicky – do you mind if I call you Nicky? – let's go somewhere where we can talk about it.'

I was taken through to a smoky office lit by flickering strip lights and crammed with desks and steel cabinets. Box files were piled against the yellowed wall and behind the grey window blinds a pale spider plant was slowly dying. A sweet old lady sat typing away at some report, the stack of Manila folders on her desk partly obscuring a full ashtray. Above her head there hung a gilded portrait of the Queen and a Metropolitan Police calendar. Her Majesty was gripping hold of a corgi dog, pressing the poor creature into the folds of her pleated tartan skirt.

I took this to be a symbol of benevolent authority: I was in the hands of a caring and wise administration.

Whitely and I sat and began our business. Over the next hour or so conversation became questioning, concern a subtle drift towards accusations of intent and pre-meditation. Later, we were joined by Detective Sergeant Oldfellow, a paunchy red-faced man who seemed to have less time for me.

'You do realise that arson is a serious offence, don't you?' he scowled.

I could only shrug in response. And then the blank statement forms were pulled from a drawer and a crown-issue biro handed to me. As I compulsively fingered a spot pulsing away on my left ear lobe and incriminated myself with the leaky pen, Whitely and Oldfellow worked their way through a packet of Rothmans king-size and provided guidance as to how I should phrase my statement. Each crushed-out fag marked another paragraph and more time pending. I joined in with the smoking, tugging on my Capstan full-strengths while filling in the details that would be used as evidence against me.

Two hours later the job was done. Whitely and Oldfellow read the statement back to me and we all declared ourselves satisfied with the good work.

'Do you want a cup of tea, Nicky?' asked Whitely.

I did and the old lady got up and switched on an electric kettle sitting on top of some green metal filing cabinets.

'Sugar?'

'Yes please,' I replied. 'Two please.'

'There won't be any sugar in the tea where you're going,' the old lady suddenly growled. Embarrassed, I glanced round the room and saw that Oldfellow and Whitely were looking at each other and grinning.

After being formally charged I was taken down into the station's basement and placed in a cell, its walls painted a cream gloss. There was a glass-brick window high in the wall opposite the door, through which I could see someone's legs moving backwards and forwards across the car park behind the station building. A bed topped with a drab green blanket and pillow resting on a tear-proof one-inch thick mattress rested along one wall.

'We'll be back for you as soon as we've spoken to your dad,' Whitely said. 'I don't see you having any trouble getting bail and you should be home tonight, OK?'

The cell door closed and I sat back, lit a Capstan and listened to the sound of traffic out on the Great North Road. Eventually I lay down and slept.

I woke to the buzzing electric light, had a piss and pressed the bell-button set in the wall in the corner by the door. After a while I heard a door open somewhere along the corridor outside.

'What do you want?' a voice yelled out.

I put my face close to the cool metal of the cell door.

'I'm waiting for my dad. He's supposed to be coming to bail me out.'

'It's a bit late for that, mate,' the voice replied. 'It's two o'clock in the morning. Get some sleep. You'll need it. You're in court in the morning.'

Bewildered, I lay down on the bed and felt something heavy and dark fall through the trap door that had opened in my stomach.

Morning brought breakfast on a polystyrene tray: toast, egg and bacon with a mug of sweet tea delivered by a cheery copper. The traffic noise was much louder now and sunlight refracted through the glass bricks of the window, filling the cell with a fool's-gold ambience. I put on my shoes and smoked and waited. After a while I heard voices followed by footsteps descending the staircase at the end of the corridor. A chain jangled and the door handle turned with a loud pop. There stood DC Whitely with two young uniformed coppers.

'Morning, Nicky. Sorry you ended up staying the night. We tried to sort out your bail but it looks like you're gonna have to go to court first.'

'I thought my old man was gonna come and bail me. That's what you said.'

Whitely gave me a thin smile. 'Yeah, well, setting fire to your neighbour's is pretty serious, mate. Let's see what the magistrates say first, eh?'

The two uniformed guys entered my cell.

'Have you got any property to bring with you?' the first of them asked.

I didn't understand and looked at Whitely.

'No. He's all right,' he said. 'Only his fags and some change and stuff. It's all been signed for.'

I picked up my Capstans and my watch from the floor by the bed and glanced around the cell to see whether I'd forgotten anything.

'Come on, mate, we haven't got all day,' the second copper

said, holding out a pair of handcuffs. As they clicked shut around my bony wrists I suppressed a rising urge to shout and kick and fight. I was led out into the corridor, one of the coppers gripping my right shoulder, the other following close behind. A sergeant walked alongside us down the corridor and opened a door leading out into the car park. The moist cool air hit me immediately; it had been raining during the night. As we descended a ramp towards the waiting police van, the copper holding my arm slipped and fell heavily, his hand loosening its grip on my shoulder as he tried to stop his face from hitting the wet concrete. The copper behind us leapt forward and grabbed my left elbow tightly, angrily twisting my arm forward as if I had somehow had something to do with the accident.

'You all right?' he asked his mate.

'Yeah. Fucking engine oil.'

He picked himself up and brushed off the small black pieces of tarmac embedded in his hand before resuming his grip – now tighter – on my arm.

'Are you all right?' I asked, hoping my question would show my wards that I was a decent fellow, that there were no bad feelings on my part.

'What the fuck's it got to do with you?' the first copper said, tightening his hold on my arm.

As we approached the rear of the van I decided to make another attempt at conversation.

'Where are we going?' I asked.

'To Highgate magistrates,' the copper behind us answered impatiently. 'Now shut up and get in.'

Arm Twister unlocked the back of the van and I climbed in and sat down on the stamped steel bench that ran the length of the compartment as the door shut behind me, leaving me in the dark.

The van rocked slightly as the policemen clambered on board and a moment later the engine started and we manoeuvred out of the yard and onto the Great North Road. My view of the world outside was restricted to what I could see through a little four-inch square portal set into the bulwark separating me from the coppers so I leaned forward and looked through this.

'Will I get bail when we get to court?' I asked.

They both burst out laughing.

'Will he get bail, he says,' said Arm Twister, his face turning towards my viewing hole.

'Will he get bail?' the other copper echoed, triggering a new round of guffaws and theatrical knee-slapping.

4

PINNER HILL

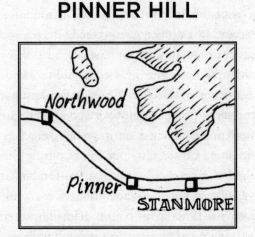

THEY TOWER EVER CLOSER to the nicotine-stained ceiling, these moth-eaten and mouldering stacks of books: Geoffrey Grigson's *The Shell Book of Roads*; Donald Maxwell's *New Lights of London; Soils and Manures* by E.J. Russell; *Hampstead Hill* co-authored by J. Logan Lobley and others; books on fungi illustrated by Beatrix Potter; crazed topographies on places of marginal interest like High Wycombe; elegant informniacs published by the Metropolitan Water Board; *Evening News* hiking guides churned out by Fieldfare in the 1950s; whole series of popular County Guides focusing on churches, stately homes and assorted 'worthies';

London Transport walking guides illustrated with wood-cuts; arcane accounts of agriculture in the home counties; Middlesex County Council records of egg-laying competitions in the 1920s; official documents celebrating the opening of swimming pools or hospitals; books on gardening, suburban architecture and lost railways, vaporised villages and destitute craftsmen, gypsies, mammals and fish.

Dozens of Kilner jars line my shelves, each packed with arte-facts gleaned from walks: a cork fishing float found in a ditch near Heathrow Airport; a Senior Service cigarette card depict-ing a missel thrush perched on a branch, plucked from the pavement in Smug Oak; a test-tube full of purple glitter filched from the shed of a derelict house near Watford. There are lead figurines – fusiliers or goats – and miniature corn dollies; Polish bookmarks made from strips of celluloid film impressed with edelweiss; stale lipsticks found in rotting handbags hidden in attics. Each is a trace, each a testimony.

Rolled maps are piled untidily in the study corner: a twelve-inch to one-mile spreadsheet of the villages to the north of west-central Scarp, including Ridge, South Mimms and Well End circa 1903, bought from the London Borough of Barnet archive; I also own a Middlesex County Council map of the East and West Main Drainage Schemes (1962); an Eastern Electricity Board 'NorthMet' diagram of the network of high-tension wires hung across London's northern fringe (1954); and dozens of six-inch to one-mile maps of the streets and houses, parks and manufactories of my home London borough (1965).

It was a first edition of Walter W. Druett's *The Stanmores and Harrow Weald Through the Ages* (1938), bought from a charity shop in Edgware in 1999, that alerted me to the possibility that the supposedly dull, annoyingly smug areas of suburbia I wandered through two or three times a week on my walks actually had their own resonant histories. Gradually the arch-sneer I carried with me whenever I walked was replaced by a deeper contemplation. A sense of stewardship rose in me where before there had been mere cynicism or even jealousy. My reading of two further books by Druett, *Harrow Through the Ages* (1949) and *Pinner Through the Ages* (1953), elevated the author in my mind to an all-seeing tutelary spirit hanging over this whole belt of Metroland strung along Scarp's southern edge. Eventually I decided that my true role in life – aside from whatever menial job I could obtain given my somewhat chequered past – was to repeatedly visit these ostensibly undistinguished pockets of human life and act as an unofficial recorder, a crow-man picking over the ruins, pulling free the anguished missals, black-bordered death notices and final demands of human life.

I began to assemble my library of specialist studies on the geography and history of my region sometime in the final years of the last century. Over the following decade I scoured the second-hand bookshops of Middlesex and Hertfordshire for dusty volumes, papers and maps, local authority guides and postcards. I visited financially imploding local studies centres – victims of a growing philosophy in local government whereby all departments had to economically justify their continued existence – for rarities on sale at knock-down prices.

I grew to care enormously for surviving pockets of plant life threatened by development; micro-colonies of woodland species hanging on desperately in the corners of parks or gardens and providing a direct link back to records made in the nineteenth and early twentieth centuries. I spent a season photographing exotic and rare species of tree and bush planted by urban and rural district councils in honour of the coronation of King George VI, guided in my efforts by a book titled *The Royal Record*, which systematically itemised such things. Why I did this, I don't know.

My study – a spare bedroom in my council flat in the Granville Road Estate, Childs Hill – became a time-capsule and time-*machine* rolled into one. Whether it was an irreplaceable gold mine or a health-hazard festering on the sharp edge of eternity I couldn't say.

There are the personal documents too: a diary kept by a nurse in 1972 in which she claims she was married to Aristotle Onassis (found in a derelict house in Leytonstone – I remember there was a tree growing in the kitchen); xeroxed pages from *Condition 23*, a collection of ruminations written by a Polish soldier just after the Second World War (pulled from a skip opposite the Finchley Memorial Hospital in 2008); a handwritten account of a crash diet found together with an NHS brochure on the best way to use Benzedrine (picked from a summer house at Slowman's Farm, 1995 – the graph charting weight loss indicated no great success). The collections of letters and photos I picked up over the years from skips or houses deserted by death spill from shoeboxes and slide across the floor until they bleed into one another. My own collection of forlorn love letters dating from a failed relationship in the 1990s joins them so that, were I to die suddenly and be found months or years later, the officials bearing the responsibility of informing my next of kin would be hard-put to identify me. And this is as it should be: I'm not Nick Papadimitriou; I am Middlesex.

I pull my region closer, dragging its leaf-fall, scrap-iron, blotting-paper substance home with me after every walk. I spread my finds out on the trestle table and spend long evenings in examination. I hear voices hovering around these tiny fragments of other times, other people's lives, though what is said and who's had who I can't often tell. The thought that anything, any event, should be overlooked horrifies me. The spot where a blackbird died, its neck snapped by a wayward football 1968 is a hallowed place; the ants' nest you exterminated down by the rose bush 1966 is the scene of a war crime.

At such times my thoughts stretch out beyond my localised identity and enter the broader field of the environment in all its complexity and arbitrariness. Though I have sympathy with Green issues and the Deep Ecology movement, the cherishing I feel is not to be reduced to these political and philosophical viewpoints. If anything, I favour the hard-science papers on ecology I read in the British Library: these well-measured and calibrated records of changes in specific plant communities dating back to the era of A.G. Tansley in the 1920s seem closer to my concerns, fine-detailed witness statements regarding what once was.

I habitually write up my thoughts in a stack of old Boots scribbling diaries – 1955, 1963, 1966 – found during an exploratory walk undertaken along a Metropolitan Water Board water main in the summer of 2003 with the psychogeographer John Rogers and the photographer Peter Knapp.

But to what avail, all this litter, these spiderweb cardboard suitcases and biscuit tins packed with junk? I always approach my chosen subject from a position of near total ignorance. Examining an Edwardian suburb, a complex network of manorial boundaries or an industrial corridor on the margins of a market town, I'm faced with and threatened by an awful blankness. I hardly know what it is I'm looking at and in spite of all the effort expended on getting to know and understand the deep topography of my region I never seem to gain the accretion of knowledge that would enable me to declare myself an expert. However often I swan in like some dishevelled, smoke-infested Richard Mabey of the buddleia set, I forget the names of plants and have to relearn them every year. I squint short-sightedly at small brown birds flapping in hedges, my lips gibbering as I attempt to name them. Rivers and parish boundaries slide around in my mind and become a squirled nightmare of shifting lines and borders. Names of historic figures slip down through the sluice gate into the main drainage scheme of my mind. It's a bastard.

But while knowledge of structure or nomenclature can foreground discreet aspects of a place, it can also occlude. Sensory properties of locations encountered while visiting or passed through – a particular moist wind that flaps about the face like a flannel, a singular quality of light remembered but seldom encountered – are screened out all too easily if the primary focus is on the type of cornicing found on a building passed or the names of the building companies that transmuted field parcels into batches of housing back in the 1930s. Which aspect of the experiential field serves as the *sine qua non* for understanding a place? For me this question has never been adequately answered.

I drift west from my tower block on a whim, sliding through the communal car park in disgust, before heading down an alley and over the Hendon Way. I cross the footbridge by Staples Corner, where Watling Street meets the North Circular and pass through the wavering fields of late summer vetches by the Welsh Harp. I probe through dismal zones of housing and sports fields and finally, just to the east of Harrow-on-the-Hill, I turn north, following a tributary of the Wealdstone Brook to where Sheepcote Farm once stood. Now it is part of the Northwick Park Hospital complex. What I have in mind is developing a keener sense of the Metroland suburbs that lap up against Scarp's southern face between Northwood Hills and Pinner.

When I was young I sneered at the suburbs. I enjoyed (and tried to write) poems that mocked what I imagined to be the stultifying tedium of suburban life. My early writings were peopled by myopic and balding clerk-like characters; pinstriped commuters gripping their briefcases on the 5.15; pearl-set lushes with eyes fixed on the tight buttocks of their gardener as he bends over the roses. Wife-swapping parties in Purley;

lumbering middle-aged encounters in the fragrant bedrooms of Gerrards Cross or Esher: these were my meat and gravy. It was an (imagined?) social roundelay I both condemned and would've given my right eye to have been part of: though I was loath to admit it, I yearned to live in the Tropic of Ruislip.

All the while, though, something else nagged at me. The more folkloric aspects of suburban house design; the way the much derided stockbroker belt was interpenetrated by relics of earlier land use; the glimpses of fields or woods visible through gaps in the semi-detacheds: all these suggested to me an organic interface between the human world and processes of longer and deeper duration. Though I told myself I wanted to leave home and go and live the swirling phantasmagoric 1970s lifestyle in London (an aspiration that was arrested when *I* was arrested and subsequently imprisoned in 1975), I was in fact torn in two, wanting on the one hand to ridicule the ribbon developments and damn the dormitory towns, and on the other hand, desiring the security I thought ownership of a house in one of these places could impart.

I head north along some modernist roadway and can see ahead the now familiar contours of Scarp. Houses climb its slope, growing more spaced out and larger the closer to the top they become. Finally I hit Uxbridge Road, which runs in parallel with Scarp all the way from Stanmore in the east to Northwood, a synthetic suburb established in the wake of the extension of the Metropolitan Railway to Rickmansworth in the 1860s.

I wanted to tell you about these towns – Pinner, Hatch End, Northwood Hills, Northwood – granting you a glimpse of their inscape, but, truth be told, I can't be bothered. Yes, they are easily subjected to abuse, their names cited in that droll, pubby English way that refuses to recognise that everywhere is somewhere: 'I heard a jumbo jet crashed into Pinner . . . and it was a month before anyone noticed.' And yes, it is my duty to elevate them to expression, perhaps composing a complex cubist poetry that codifies their crystalline facets, their fault-lines and their unconscious impulses, but today is not the day.

As I wander west along Uxbridge Road it all looks too big to even begin to take on. There are large and small houses, blue and black cars, shoe shops, schools and a particularly ornate arts centre at Hatch End. I cross streams running under the road, tributaries of the Pinn and the Yeading, and – as I approach Oxhey Lane, which runs off to the north, Watford Bound – I see the termini of two separate sections of Scarp, the Oxhey Wood–Pinner segment which declines in the east towards the valley of the Hertsmere Brook, and the western bulge of the Harrow Weald–Stanmore sector, rising like the haunch of a giant sleeping dog above the suburban belt.

And what of it? Today terminus is everywhere and I feel precisely nothing. Perhaps it's the summer heat or the large lunch I had before setting off but there's no blood in my brain, no near-frenzied pleasure. I'm left with flat fact and nothing else.

Finally, I make it to Northwood, turning north up Hallowell Road for Northwood Underground. Just before I enter the teeming shopping parade I sit on a wall and try to visualise what it would be like if I were feeling more responsive, if I did feel capable of entering the inner lives of the Scarp townships.

I imagine sometimes that I'm on a powerful and as yet undiscovered hallucinogen, one that dissolves the ego-boundaries so effectively that subject and object fuse, so that, were I to ingest this substance while visiting Northwood, I would in some way pass into and become the suburb's main thoroughfare. It would be a multiplex, transtemporal experience, my usual self reduced to a residual monad blabbing in a conflagration of women, men and the billions of objects large and small that surround them and which define their business. I'm bonded solidly into the sun-heated architrave of a multi-storey car park and then become the raw face of a shop assistant smoking a fag in the accommodation road behind Bowley's shoe shop 3 March 1997; I see through the eyes of a young girl serving tea at the Gondola café 8 May 2007, savour the pleasure of both parties enjoying a quick knee-trembler behind the London Bible College, 14 June 1965. Your story is one among many as you surge through from Ruislip by bus for work at the Regal Kebab and Fish Bar. It is 1995 and I'm back from Poland, drunk on Special Brew at 7 a.m. cutting through from Watford to Oxhey and along river-parks to the ancillary margins of all this woogle-wagging yeah-yeah-yeah and wooh-wooh-wooh. I probably passed you at a bus stop or hair salon. I was well muttering by then, torn by your Middlesex lives, your towers eerie across landscapes, your madness of A roads and zooty careerists canoodling in cars by Batchworth Golf Club.

I call this experience *prakrti-laya*, a yogic term derived from the ancient Indian Samkhya philosophy. *Prakrti-laya* is described in Georg Feuerstein's *Encyclopedic Dictionary of*

Yoga as 'absorption into nature'. Feuerstein goes on to cite the *Yoga Sutra*'s view, that *prakrti-laya* is a 'pseudo-liberation'. If this is so, well, I don't care anyway. Being a topographer I'm fatally attached to this earth and when I die I will be bound here, destined to burn-out with the planet at the end of its lifespan. To repeat, I don't care. Do you? Rather this thin enlightenment than a rationalist state of grace born of a conclusive map of the soul or some other arrogant construct. You can take your concern for 'spirituality' and 'appropriacy' and shove it, mister! I'm on my way out; I'm on my way in.

So these buses discharging crowds of shoppers on wet Tuesdays in November 1991 outside Northwood's tube station; these warm-lit pubs packed with botoxed Middlesex wild-life; these muscular and tattooed geezers with their receding hairlines and shirts hanging out of their tight trousers; these gaggles of schoolgirls on the pull and women whose histories are endlessly recycled to the latest bespectacled dullard sitting and nodding understandingly in the futile hope of some action some time, some year, some century, until life has passed and it is all too late: they come to me now both as mass and in individual detail in my *prakrti-laya*, breaking me so thoroughly that beads of sweat appear on my brow despite the cold. I am a weirdo unwelcome in culturally inclusive public libraries; I sit alone, sopping and slobbering, and read local authority hand-books published circa 1962 on shitty rainy day playing fields.

The streets creep up Scarp's south slope becoming less pocked, plastered and stitched the higher they climb. Each house is a mediating station refracting the land's current, binding its energies into table lamps, pink bathroom tiles and electric coffee grinders. There are flush lavatories, bare arses and hair extensions. There are endless conversations filling planetary time, and a soft tearing departure from reality.

In the final analysis, what can be said about these endless-seeming streets, most of which I have never visited and where I know no one? Yes, there are cars parked everywhere; perhaps the locals are venal by and large; who cares? And why would I want to come on like some two-bit psychogeographer, a myopic and beaked monstrosity eager to impress with my architectural knowledge, my eye for the telling detail? So often something is delivered up on walks, but not today.

I push my notebook down into my jacket pocket and put away my camera. There is really nothing to say, so I turn away, my head hung in defeat, and start for home. A mile later I pass through a greasy patch of sports field adjacent to the Metropolitan Railway near Kenton. Suddenly my attention is drawn to an astonishing sight: a hedgehog, its head firmly wedged in a plastic yoghurt carton, is running round in small panicked circles on the tarmac path a few feet ahead. I can hear it snuffling as it struggles to breathe, can sense the terror in its blind rush. Leaning forward, I pull the suffocating mask free from the tiny animal's head. Hi, I'm the region and I love you, I want to say. Is there any recognition, any thanks? The hedge-hog, its face smeared with strawberry yoghurt, looks up at me, blinks once or twice and then immediately curls into a ball. I make a gesture of kicking this small morsel with whom I share the planet over towards a goal-mouth a few yards off and then lean forward to take a closer look at the little fellow. The experience has made my day but there is no thanks at the end of it, no appreciation of my perceptiveness or concern. Such is the way.

*

Arm Twister was ranting on about how the Criminal Injuries Board had paid him next to nothing for an injury to his knee, 'suffered in the furtherance of my duty', as he put it with some difficulty. Apparently some woman he'd arrested had kicked him hard on his shin after he called her a slag. His mate made sympathetic sounds – a policeman's lot is not a happy one, etc. I listened to them both, perhaps hoping to learn something useful, but soon grew tired of hearing of the depredations that, from their own account, they routinely handed out. With their pork-flesh faces, their serge uniforms and their polished leather belts laden with rubberised and toughened-plastic accoutrements, they were just too damn different. My hair hadn't been washed for six months; I had bad acne; and my jeans flared far beyond reasonable bounds – I was clearly going to be nothing other than an object of hatred to them. Besides, something else was on my mind: as the police van began to climb towards East Finchley, I pressed my face closer to the portal and stared at the all-too-familiar buildings I could see approaching: an Edwardian parade of shops; the Rex Cinema (now the Phoenix), where I saw the Beatles starring in *Help!* back in 1965; Eric Aumonier's art-deco Archer standing gracefully on his plinth to the side of the steel railway bridge that carries the Northern Line over the Great North Road. I shifted my left cheek to the left side of the portal and tried to gain a glimpse of the three ten-storey council-built tower-blocks at Prospect Ring, over to the van's right. I was determined to get a final view of these before I disappeared from the world, for how long no one knew.

A couple of years previously I had 'fallen in love' with a girl, whom I shall refer to simply as D——, who was in the year below me at school. At that time I had a job in the school library and after working out which class she was in from where she stood during our occasional playground fire drills, I dipped into some files my official status gave me access to and discovered her full name and address.

I had to know the world D—— inhabited and so one freezing November evening in 1974 I left home and walked the mile and a half to East Finchley, guided to her street by the *A–Z* stuffed into my coat pocket. Turning off the High Road close to the Bald Faced Stag, I passed through a council estate consisting of three tower blocks and an asbestos-roofed youth club. 'Lucky, the dwellers of these blocks, to be so close to her,' I thought as I slipped down a concrete-slatted alleyway (a graffito: *Dimond Dogs*) and over a footbridge that crossed the snowy underground line. A red tube train of 1938 stock sparked as it emerged from a tunnel, the snow muffling the sound of its wheels rattling against the stone-cold rails. It pulled into the station and I paused to watch the passengers ooze out of the carriages and descend the stairs before dispersing to their warm homes. All this electricity, this funky democratic energy and city-movement swinging from the hips of office girls! I was entering a vortex; I was zoning in on D——'s world.

Her street was a cul-de-sac on the edge of the Hampstead Garden Suburb, the entrance to which was along a short stretch of road divided down its centre by a small green upon which several wooden posts stood, supporting a spiked ornamental chain. Beyond this the road split; one arm turned away to the right and then curved left to form a circle, completing its circuit by emerging from behind some smart four-square houses that made my heart sink as soon as I saw them. Classic specimens of what we used to call mock Tudor, they spoke of a wealth and privilege far beyond my reach. I knew immediately that I didn't – would never – have the right credentials to pass through their broad front doors into the sumptuous worlds lived within. I was simply out-classed; a dirty-faced boy, with my nose pressed to the toyshop window while my precious few coppers rattled in my pockets.

My heart thumping, I counted off the house numbers and closed on my quarry with some haste as if I was returning after a lengthy and enforced absence to a place lovingly remembered. However, finally seeing D——'s house gave me no joy. In fact, it merely dealt my dreams a further savage blow. Detached and even larger than the other houses in the street, it stood in a broad and deep front garden. Everything about her house – the garage with its shiny aluminium door, the wild roses growing on an arched lead trellis over the gate, the ornate wrought-iron pipes and gutters – told me that it would never welcome the likes of me. The chunky brass knocker hanging from the carefully painted front door granted access to circles in which I could never move. In my mind I could see the wine-wise young barristers, the hirsute and handsome middle-class musicians who undoubtedly populated D——'s world languidly entering or leaving the place. The windows, dark and inscrutable but clearly fitted with good solid locks, were perfect symbols of my exclusion. I was particularly drawn to a single window immediately above the front door, which suggested to me a small bedroom, possibly hers. As I stood there in the freezing air my mind feverishly conjured up scenes in which D——'s hair fanned across a fine duck-feather pillow as the hated face of an imagined rival gazed down on her, his self-satisfied eyes shining with lust and triumph.

Dismayed, I wandered off for another look around the cul-de-sac, expecting nothing other than further humiliations, more thumbs down from the jury in attendance. The carefully spaced houses, each distinct yet bearing a strong family resemblance; the gardens with their ornamental wells and fountains of pampas grass; curbs lined with polished cars: everything about the street seemed meticulously placed, occupying its correct position by divine decree. Even the street lamps and the green telephone junction box over by the entrance to an alleyway seemed to hum with an energy that flowed down from some higher plane. It was difficult to believe that a finite number of footsteps trudged along pavements from my dog-eared streets could, by increments, have led to this cynosure embedded in the heart of London N2.

Yet there were dualities, divisions and complexities even here. The cul-de-sac told me a tale of two different worlds. On the one hand there were the large garages with their frictionless push-up/pull-down doors (very 1970s), the outsized and portentous neo-classical colonnades and entablatures and the subdued orange or pink lighting glimpsed through diamond-latticed windows. These symbolised the world D—— inhabited, with its leather-seated cars and professional self-confidence. Yet beneath all this there ran a mysterious counter-current, as if the older world upon which all this wealth had been lacquered continued to exert its influence: a yew tree growing in its own miniature wayside garden in a tiny side road; the ornate stone bird table in a front garden; the houses themselves, with their black-braced jetties and elaborate brick-nogging suggestive of the age of Shakespeare and John Dee: these were portals that spanned deep-time, cobwebbed doorways, built into the very fabric of the place, which opened onto ethereal fields and woods, mythological and fabled gods and beasts; the noble and timeless tattoo of plant lore.

It was past midnight now and as the snow, which had begun to fall lightly, changed to icy rain, I turned up my collar, lit a Capstan, and stood, feeling like a poet, beneath a street lamp. I was waiting for something to happen but was unable to work out what exactly.

Nothing happened and come 2 a.m. I was ready to set off home. I was tired, the rain pricked my scalp and my face felt greasy and wan. I decided to leave a votive offering and, feeling around in my pockets, I found a betting-shop biro and a cheap gold-painted cigarette case my mum had given me. I opened this and pulled out my last two fags, pocketing them. I wrote some now forgotten message on the textured inner face of the case and left it lying on her garden path. It was all I could do.

I had begun to walk off when suddenly a motorbike came whining around the corner. It halted outside her house and the pillion rider – recognisably a female, even at this distance – dismounted, spoke briefly to the motorcyclist and began to walk up the garden path as the bike pulled away. I froze in terror, standing in the middle of the road barely fifty yards away. What if she saw me? And when she found the cigarette case? What then? Though terrified, I was nevertheless unable to turn my eyes away from what followed. As D——, her helmet now tucked under her arm, passed through the garden gate and approached the front door she stopped and bent down. She straightened up and seemed to be examining something in the orange light cast by the street lamp that stood by her garden gate. I saw a frown crease her face. My blood pounded in my head and I felt as if I were trembling on the edge of utter disaster. Then she shrugged and entered her house briskly, the door slamming behind her. Moments later a light went on in the upstairs room. As I made the long cold walk home, it occurred to me that what had been truly enthralling about the whole experience was not so much the close encounter with D—— as my intense exposure to the street in which she lived.

After that I returned to the cul-de-sac nearly every week, usually at night. Despite the horror it invoked in me, each visit left me feeling as if I had moved closer to the edge of some elusive and mysterious knowledge. When I lay on my bed smoking afterwards, I would imagine the vastness of the city smeared across the curve of the Earth's surface. There was the brightly lit centre full of fine restaurants and galleries blazing with ingenious art. There was suburbia with its well-trimmed parks and wide-windowed modern schools. The arterial roads, factories and poor sections of town had their place also. Finally, there was the 'countryside', as manifested in the ring of green surrounding the bulk of the city. There was all of this and – right at the heart of this living system – there was this little cul-de-sac.

Arm Twister's mate brought the van to a sudden lurching stop opposite East Finchley Station.

'Stupid Jewish cow!' he shouted. 'Did you see that?'

'Yeah. Bloody women drivers!' Arm Twister replied, shaking his head. 'They've got no idea.'

Arm Twister looked round at me. 'And what are you bloody well looking at?' he snapped as he lifted a flap and slammed it shut over my own little portal, sealing me in.

We left East Finchley behind us and began to climb the Great North Road uphill towards Highgate. Arm Twister had robbed me of my forward view so I turned instead to the window set in the door at the back of the van and watched my world recede behind me. We passed Cherry Tree Wood, its bare winter oaks visible through a gated entrance. I remembered my sister telling me that she once saw Ray Davies of the Kinks drinking a cup of tea in the café in the woods. It must've been sometime in the autumn of 1970. I thought back to that time and how, even then, there was an evident decline in standards, as if the world had come out of the 1960s with a sulk because the parties were no longer such fun, the main players both ageing and drifting into the broader largo of their addictions. I looked out at the tired hippy masses thronging the high street, the disappointed faces of women emerging from Bishops Avenue. A bell-bottomed soul boy pissed against a brick buttress supporting the ivy-laden embankment carrying the tube railway towards Highgate Hill. It's all going to be washed away, I thought. Its time is coming and what'll happen to us all I don't know.

We passed some wide-windowed modern blocks of flats set back in their communal gardens and drives. Their concrete balconies were rain-drenched and bare. The mottled plane trees that lined the road had ditched their sopping leaves over the cars parked outside. We stopped at a traffic light and a line of vehicles queued up behind us. A haggard-faced woman sitting in a green Renault picked her nose and muttered to herself as she leaned over the steering wheel to grab a tissue from the glove compartment, a magic-tree car freshener dangling in front of her. I wondered whether she'd noticed me staring out at her but somehow doubted it. We were in separate worlds now. The light changed and we resumed our climb. Finally the road levelled out and then dropped slightly as it approached the junction with the Archway Road. We shifted into a new traffic lane and the road up to Highgate disappeared behind some shabby brick houses set in gardens, their privet hedges greyed with the silt deposited by heavy traffic. We passed small derelict cottages and the bulging green presence of Highgate Wood on my right as I looked backwards. I wished I was in there, among the palsied horn-beams, the earthy mushroom smells and the sounds of rain ticking off the laurel leaves rather than stuck here, new prop-erty of Her Majesty's government.

We turned off the main road into a side street, and then again into a courtyard behind the 1950s police station and magistrates' court. Arm Twister got out the van and rang a bell mounted in the wall by a plain wooden door. It opened to reveal a bitter-looking man in uniform, his belt weighted with a large selection of keys. The van door opened. 'Out', Arm Twister said, and I stepped down from the van into cold air and, passing through the door, descended a small flight of steps into a long narrow corridor buzzing with strip lights and smell-ing of urine, Dettol and tobacco. As the turnkey opened a cell door and told me to get in I asked him if my dad was in court.

'I dunno, mate. You'll have to speak to your solicitor about that.'

'I haven't got a solicitor,' I replied.

'Well, you're fucked, then,' the turnkey said as he pulled the door shut in my face.

Looking round I saw the now-familiar flecked cream walls, wooden bench and stone tiling underfoot. I sighed, sat and lit a cigarette, waiting for something to happen.

I listened to the sounds coming from the corridor, trying to gauge the situation I now found myself in, the procedures and processes whereby my immediate future would be shaped. Every now and then a voice would shout out a name from the end of the corridor and then I would track the movement of the turnkey as he walked along the corridor. There would be the sound of the key turning in a heavy steel lock and then the crack as the handle was pulled to open up. Next, soft voices would be heard passing as the prisoner and the turnkey headed towards the stairs leading to the courtroom. It was all so familiar somehow, as if custodial environments offer so little in terms of stimulus that I had gleaned a basic feel for their ambience from watching a handful of police serials on television back in the 1960s. I sensed that rather than being a mere interlude before returning to my former life, my pending court appearance was merely the first step on a longer and darker journey, one that would carry me far from the streets and houses of my world into landscapes both unsettling and – I hoped against reason – rewarding.

Looking up I saw a light bulb glowing behind a square of tough Perspex sheet mounted into the ceiling. It crossed my mind to hang myself but my laces and belt had been taken from me at Whetstone police station and anyway I couldn't find anywhere in the cell where I could've gained purchase. Bored, I settled back on the bench, curled up to retain body heat and began to succumb to the weary numbness that closed on my mind like a coarse grey prison blanket.

I woke to the sound of keys rattling and the door being pushed open.

'Solicitor,' the turnkey snapped and I sat up. A tall slender man in a flared charcoal pinstripe suit entered and, raising his eyebrows enquiringly, leaned forward awkwardly and shook my hand. His smoothly shaved and intelligent face was topped by a bouffant; his shoes were black and buckled.

'Nick, is it?'

'Yeah.'

'I'm David Cope from Skewers and Tregaskis. The court has asked me to represent you.'

'Oh right. Is my dad here? He's supposed to be getting me bail.'

'I . . . don't think so,' David replied, shuffling some papers uneasily, 'He'll probably show up next time you're in court.'

'Next time? But I live with him,' I said, my voice rising in panic.

'Well, yes, I mean, you'll be able to see him when you get home,' David answered, looking increasingly uncomfortable.

'So I'll get bail then?'

'Oh, I expect so. Look, can you fill in these forms for me? They're an application for legal aid. I can't represent you unless they're signed.'

'And then I'll get bail?'

'Er, yes, I expect so,' David said, rising and heading for the cell door. 'I'll see you in court in a few moments. Sign those forms.'

Then he was gone and the turnkey pulled the door shut with a smirk.

A few minutes later the turnkey unlocked me again.

'Come on. The magistrates want to see you.'

I followed him down the corridor, passing various suited figures whispering through door flaps to their clients and up some steps to where a copper stood leaning against the wall by a heavy wooden door. On the far side came the sound of murmuring and a faint smell of furniture polish, shoe wax and old papers. It was the scent of what we used to call The Establishment.

'Are they ready yet?' the turnkey said.

'No,' the copper whispered, opening the door slightly and peering through the crack.

'Will I get bail now?' I asked the copper.

He looked me up and down and grinned to the turnkey.

'I doubt it,' he said, and turned back to the door, opening it again.

'Right, we're on!' he announced finally and taking my right elbow in both hands, he opened the door and led me through.

5

STANMORE

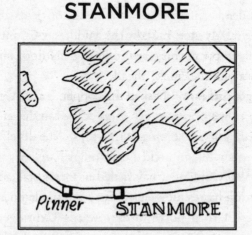

WALK UP PINNER HIGH Street and along Church Lane, to a narrow alleyway running between high fences, over the tops of which peek apple trees and shed roofs. At the alley's far end, a street of neat 1950s houses climbs directly ahead to a crest from where – at a certain point in the dead centre of the road – the land drops in every direction: southwards towards Nower Hill Cemetery with its views of the Kodak Factory and the HMSO printing works at Headstone; west over the roofs of Pinner, the church tower visible beyond; north across numerous side roads; and eastwards where a huge rampart of wooded high ground recedes dramatically into the distance. This last is the next fold of Scarp, taking in Harrow Weald and Stanmore, and it draws me like a magnet. Ahead, the road fades to a small grassy promontory overlooking a broad plateau of farmland scattered with cows and shabby farm buildings. A concrete track runs dead centre through the wedge of fields and crosses King George V Avenue, built by the Middlesex County Council in the 1930s to connect the new suburb of North Harrow with the Uxbridge Road. I move ahead.

The wind ruffles my hair as I walk the track. Calves stare out at me through tube-steel gates while shrieking flocks of ring-necked parakeets gather in tree-tops. There is electricity in the flight of swifts, an arched caterpillar hanging by a thread from an oak, cylinders of hay sealed in sheets of black plastic.

A footbridge takes me over the Euston Railway to Headstone Lane, where I turn northwards towards Uxbridge Road. A hundred yards to the right of the road junction I take a track-way that climbs Scarp towards Stanmore. To the left the fields collapse into a gulley carrying a tributary of the Pinn Brook down towards Pinner. Ahead are white farm buildings and a tumble-down barn of corrugated iron. Looking back over my shoulder I can make out the dark mass of Moor Park and the flats of the West Middlesex Market Garden Plain.

The track surfaces high up at Old Redding, a dangerously busy road running between laurel-infested woodlands and stretches of open field. Across the way, lurking deep in the foli-age, runs the vallum and fosse of Grim's Dyke, an extensive earthwork that snakes its way uphill from Pinner before dimin-ishing in height and finally disappearing on Harrow Weald

Common. Grim's Dyke runs parallel with and just to the south of the Middlesex–Hertfordshire boundary. Why and when it was built remains a point of dispute.

I carry with me an eighteen-inch Boron rod which I keep rolled in a stitched sheet of rabbit fur. Unwrapping the rod, I poke one end into the embankment and position the other to my forehead. The sound of the cars on Old Redding fades and I'm inside this snaking earthwork and become generations of azaleas first planted in 1869. I am the Wilde Beestes Wood and churning of butter in wooden pales. Hairy and fierce, I tear off my leather jerkin and rub the juice of agaric and hemlock into my temples. Now it is 1972 and I gaze fondly at the purple Volkswagen camper I've just fitted with globoid stereo speakers. I'm so of my time that even my nostrils are flared. Then my bass guitar is sold and I decay into three-piece suits, business lunches and clicking IBM file-index machines.

What is the force that generates all these steel-framed windows, the cherry blossoms erupting along streets I visited once only and never found again and the smiling lollipop lady guiding straggling groups of schoolkids to safety? I understand war better than birth and trust roadkill more than lambs or speckled eggs. I see steamrollers and workmen from the county council tamping down a modern roadway – its dual carriageways divided by islands of grass – in order to link up the pattern of streets slowly crystallising on the farm land. I see families arriving by pantechnicon, settees rumbling across newly laid paving stones, vases and plants carried by whistling removal men in brown overcoats. Then there are gaily coloured milfoils springing up in brick-edged trapezoids of compost laid by garden paths and satchel-burdened school-boys walking – and later being driven – to schools saturated with sunlight. The family picnics in the summer garden on chicken, Wonderloaf and jars of pickled peppers. A blackbird hops under the stone bench as the boys play football. Then the leaves fall and it snows. One dark day the cat becomes ill, the children crowding around her basket. Later a small mound of soil strewn with flowers appears behind the crab-apple. Then the flowers fade and dry to dust. I fall, muttering and sweat-soaked to the ground, my legs twitching and my eyeballs bulging against the aphid-specked lenses of my tortoiseshell glasses.

After dusting myself down, I strike off, tracing the ditch and embankment past astonishing sequoias, rhododendron bushes and the tile-hung and half-timbered Grim's Dyke Hotel, built in 1872 by Norman Shaw for the artist Frederick Goodall and – from 1890 – the home of the Savoy Opera librettist William Schenk Gilbert.

Just east of Grim's Dyke is Harrow Weald, a dank, gloomy wood, its slippery, mossy floor fissured by small streams feeding the Pinn. I pass through rapidly, the path chosen taking me behind a fenced-off garden centre and the site of a Roman kiln, and head towards a radio mast marking the entrance to the grounds of Bentley Priory. A striking feature of the land here is the sheer number of ant mounds scattered about on the coarse grass. Despite the general dryness of the soil, there are occasional marshy patches, indicative of the presence of moor-pan, a hard impermeable substratum of the soil consisting of clay, iron ore and small stones.

This stretch of heath-clad and wooded high ground, clearly visible from my kitchen window seven miles away, is dominated by the sprawling and campaniled mansion of Bentley Priory. During the Second World War it served as the HQ of Fighter Command. Every time I visit, I'm swamped with mental images of wartime Britain that seem bound to this landscape, though perhaps they really originate from films seen as a child. Caped nurses with Home Counties accents chat on the short walk to the nursing station; grey-uniformed air force personnel smoke at the striped barrier by the guard hut; suave and brilliantined controllers in air-raid plotting sheds issue clipped instructions to Hurricane pilots somewhere over Kent. The whole of southern England is sucked in on the airwaves to be condensed down to pale-green blips on a circular screen. With a 'tally-ho', fighters fly in formation over Harefield. Then there is a triumphant shout as a Dornier ploughs into the trees at Moor Park and explodes. Lord Air Chief Dowding coughs and sprinkles salt on his Woolton Pie. A smart young aide approaches, salutes and passes him a report. Later, urgent discussions on air strategy take place somewhere deep within the sprawling Victorian building.

The whole of Stanmore seems to be imbued with this sense of the past. The shiny modern cars driving down Warren Lane on the far side of the Mansion are out of time with the place, roaring about like impudent and vulgar young upstarts gatecrashing an otherwise solemn social event.

Looking south from the roof of a pillbox in which I have been known to sleep occasionally, I can see the trio of tower blocks marking the estate in which I live, far off in Childs Hill. I think of my three cats, doomed by my caring to spend their whole lives living in the gaps between these slabs of pebble-dashed high-density housing. Even as I sit and squint through my binoculars, trying to make out the curtains in my living-room window, they are sunbathing on the roof of the pram-sheds next to the car park or are busy worrying the linnets down in the allotment across the road. I can see clearly from this elevation that the estate is propped halfway up the side of a hill that climbs all the way from low-lying Cricklewood to the elegant heights of Hampstead. My cats, though, will never know this – their concerns are strictly localised. But, in the final analysis, I'm no better informed than they are. We can never truly pin down where our place of dwelling lies; each newly discovered overview of what we call home effectively places it within a new topography, forcing us to redefine what it is we mean when we say 'I live there'.

I cross Stanmore cricket ground and pass the ancient fish-ponds before entering Stanmore Common. One night in 1996, after an afternoon spent picking my way through this gravel-pocked morass of tree roots, miasmic ditches and household detritus, I dreamt I saw my mother waiting by the side of Warren Lane, a narrow road that cuts across the common. She was standing in the shade cast by the trees, a wind-whipped lacework of fool's parsley seething round her ankles and calves. For some reason I knew the year was 1944 – perhaps it was her curly and thick brown hair and rosy cheeks, which made her look about fourteen years old. Suddenly a tarpaulined army lorry rattled around the corner, its brakes hissing as it pulled up next to her. The driver exchanged a few brief words with her – what about I couldn't tell – before resuming his journey. My mother watched the truck drive away and then mounted her bike and rode off in the opposite direction. When I woke I could still see her standing there, her eyes squinting in the bright sunlight as she stared at a bend in the lane.

And there are other images and voices that surface as I sneak through a recently completed luxury estate, my aim being to make my way to Borehamwood and catch the train home. There are the clicks, whistles, and rattles of flocks of starlings forming up in the trees by the pillow mound near Warren Lane before flying in to London to roost overnight on Duck Island in St James's Park. I also hear the liquid twitter of finches in the hedgerows as I work north on foot, talking loudly to myself while trying to find a route through to the A41.

And there is another feathered presence that comes to mind whenever I pass this way. I hear his laughter now as he stares down from his roost upon my momentary pleasures, my thinly disguised conceits.

*

I croak and look out across the valley from this lip of land to the grey Abbey of St Albans. Great pockets of gold shift across the levels, moving with the clouds from Otterspool, where, in thirty years' time, twenty-four-year-old Frederick Burgess of 116 Fordwych Road, West Hampstead, will die instantly after being thrown from the motorbike stolen earlier that day from outside the Red Lion pub in Childs Hill. The light slides east, spreading over Butler's Green, a relative height from which one day soon there will be views of the suburbs of Watford with their corrugated-iron bomb-shelters, their electronics, print-ing, and tube steel manufactories. But that is all in the future so I put it out of my mind; it is feed time and today I'm given nuts and yellow sultanas. I stretch my neck and bend forward and down, placing my head to one side, the better to take each morsel in my chopstick bill. Bangles click together on Mrs Brightwen's freckled forearm as she strokes my deep blue head.

The telephonic apparatus rattles and Mr Odell answers – 'Good afternoon, GRImsdyke 104' – before passing the brass mouthpiece to Mrs Brightwen; it's that tiresome Mr W.S. Gilbert again, Stanmore's only other user of the new telephone system. He's sniffing about for ideas for a new opera: perhaps a bird theme this time, don't you think? A chorus rigged out as crows and gulls? A few words exchanged and the mouthpiece is set back on its cradle. I am all bright-eyed and brainy and flash blue-electric while my lady blasts Mr Gilbert for daring to bother her with his creative dilemmas.

Don't be too hasty in condemning him, I think. Not long now and they'll be dragging his body from that lake of his over at Grim's Dyke.

I'm proud and preen myself. Sometimes I use Mr Odell's discarded cigarette ends to smoke the tics out from under my ragged wings. I really am that vain! And I have reason enough for all this pride because I know what's coming, I have already seen it happen; I am something other than these temporally localised big-brained dominant bipeds with their wireless telegraphs and armoured cruisers, their crappers and newfangled internal combustion engines. I am something other than Blanche, Mrs Brightwen's adorable white dove, or her brown owl, Asnapper. The African antelope grazing in the long grass over by the tulip tree; the lemur, tugging his striped tail as he sits on the bookshelf by the stairs: they don't get it either. I am something other than any living thing I have ever known.

Mrs Brightwen sits in the sun by The Hunge, a large mound of earth once reckoned to be Queen Boudicca's grave, though I know this is not true. The earthwork is laden with hollyhocks, flannels and puddingstones – erratics bonded by hardened ferric salt. They were carried south to this land by ice-sheets only last week it seems – and writes in her ornate 'animal diary' as I perch on her shoulder and tinker with her earrings. The black ditches are specked with fallen blossom slowly moving north with the water downhill into Hertfordshire while I sit enjoying the sun. I doze and dream of wars and a human god who makes fighter planes. I see fat billowing balloons attached to earth by steel cables; I see prefab huts and anti-aircraft guns; I see endless flows of traffic, smashed bodies, squashed foxes.

I tug hard at Mrs Brightwen's left ear lobe and she turns her face towards me. 'Merops, stop that, you spiteful little bird!'

She tickles under my clever little chin and it feels so good I wheeze and flap and then ascend to the very top of the

Taxodium out of sheer joy. 'You will come back, won't you, Merops, you naughty rook?' Mrs Brightwen shouts. And I will, to be sure, but first I take the opportunity to inspect once again this long islet of upland, this scarp we inhabit.

Away the high ground runs from my perch, towards where the sun sets, where my friends at Harefield risk the farmer's shotgun to look for leather-jackets and wire-worm. I know Harefield, with its chalk downs, its almshouses, dull-witted woodpeckers and drug murders. I know of its tansy puddings and mobile phones, hens scratching in the dusty lane, whiskered rat-catchers, knocking shops and fried-chicken outlets.

Away the land runs to where the sun rises and there it is ancient woodland, black belts of hornbeam glowering across river valleys, bands of white suburbs emerging and then swept away; there are ants swarming on sticky summer afternoons and African ladybirds; green parakeets and continental hornets. Between these two bookends, so-to-say, the long ridge runs, it taking me an hour and a half to traverse from east to west.

Mrs Brightwen first took me on as a guest at The Grove after a day's such observations had left me pondering on what was and what would be. That year – 1903 – had been mildly tricky with small fires in the furze on Stanmore Common, thin wreaths of smoke winding through Mrs Brightwen's larches and horse chestnuts. Both of us knew her house and grounds would survive the flames; she through her Quaker faith, I because I see it all, past, present and future at once.

'Ah, look at you, you miserable thing,' she'd said as I

hunched on a low bough above her lawn, a full-day's worth of the land's memories having played through my mind, leaving me depleted. 'Why aren't you with your brothers and sisters in the woods? Has the rook parliament ejected you, or are you just an unfriendly little rook?'

God bless Mrs Brightwen, whose writings I knew would assure me my fame; I flashed her with my best blue-electric and flew down to rest at her feet. When I first met her she had already enjoyed considerable success with her books on natural history, beginning with the publication of *Wild Nature Won by Kindness* in 1892. My personal favourite is *Inmates of my House and Garden* (1899). Insects, flowers, plants, the mammals and, of course, birds: these were all cherished by her, all loved, both as specimens and as individuals. I fancied leaving my black tatter-feathered mark on history – an ink-splodge on the annals of time if you like – and made sure I got well in with the old dear. Besides, her house was something else again. Wide belts of beech trees surrounded the grounds and between these there grew numerous exotic species of rhododendrons. They were vastly superior to the frugal specimens you'll find today at Scratchwood and Moat Mount. There was also an avenue of cedars through which could be glimpsed (for no reason I have ever ascertained) a statue of Dick Whittington. Gardens sunken and Italian backed onto a large nectarine house. A mushroom house stood down by the main gate. The rustic gardener's bothy (where Mr Odell used to sit and smoke during quiet moments) was positioned between a large galvanised iron soft-water tank and a particularly tall cedar of

Lebanon below which there stood – again for no reason I could understand – a replica of the tomb of Jean-Jacques Rousseau. Most of all, I loved the grotto hidden in the rhododendrons by the south edge of the grounds. A current of the old religion subsisted below Mrs Brightwen's Christianity and this came to the fore whenever she entered this curious conical brick chamber with its sandstone shrine (on which she felt obliged to place a large iron crucifix). Happy the hours I spent there with Mrs Brightwen and various visitors, listening to them discuss the world of nature. It was in the grotto that she and Mr Hudson (who I will tell you about shortly) drafted plans for the petitioning of Parliament in order to outlaw the use of bird feathers in the millinery trade. In this they succeeded. The trade in cage birds was harder to beat, however, and legislation outlawing that nasty business didn't follow until long after Mrs Brightwen's death.

At the lower end of the garden, where Middlesex changes to Hertfordshire, several springs merged to form a chain of ponds before running north to the reservoir they built on Lord Aldenham's tract. Here there was an octagonal iron gatepost. (It is still there today. I once saw you walk past it; you were muttering to yourself.) It is a good place to sit and watch the times shift from ponderous giant lizards chewing their way through whole forests to lumbering and obsolescent gas-guzzlers eating up that stupid Watford by-pass.

Impressed with my knowledge? Listen, I could tell you the whole history of any one of your counties, feeding it instantaneously into your 'Lord of the Universe' brain and it would frazzle that little monkey mind of yours so thoroughly you'd end up on insulin or electric shock or sex hormone treatment in Shenley or Napsbury over yonder on the high ground beyond Radlett. I could flash blue-electric all day, communicating telepathically with ants' nests in Dacorum or Cashio, living it up in slowworm universes by the allotments at Potters Crouch (you know where I mean, of course), or accessing the memories of bargemen coming into Watford by canal from Uxbridge circa 1947.

Here's a sample: a little something lost to history (possibly through being suppressed!). That arse Geoffrey de Mandeville once set his soar sparhawk at me after I wound him up by *kaa-kaa*ing away (out of sheer vindictiveness, I hasten to add) and keeping him awake all night in his little motte-and-bailey at South Mimms. Come morning he rode out in his silk and leopard-skin finery and attended by valets to where I sat waiting for him on an alder branch by Vinegar Spring. 'Halt,' he commanded his retinue upon espying me and, summoning his swain, Asgar, took from him that poncified killer of sparrows, Leofgeat. De Mandeville clearly wasn't great with birds, for otherwise he'd have known that it's us crows who terrorise these little southern hunters and not the other way round. Just go out to any stretch of open land – say, by the gravel pits at Yeading, or some of the flat lands near Heathrow Airport – and you'll see us escorting hawks off the premises, invariably helping them on their way with the odd good hard nip or scratch. (I should add here that the herons get it from us, too: it was I who instigated the mass attack by the Wendover rookery on the Totteridge heronry in 1942. The aim was to drive the herons over to Mr Samuel Pulham's house at East Finchley and get them to empty out that butcher's fishpond. Pulham was giving us a hard time, using his status as Mayor of Finchley to promote our persecution as part of the so-called Dig for Victory campaign. Hurled sticks, catapults, even the odd shotgun or Webley .455 claimed many a corvine life that year. Oh, how we laughed as the hungry herons helped themselves to his prize carp!) The truth is that many of these windhovers, sparhawks, and such-like heraldic birds are suited for little more than the mass-murder of ring-doves at Edgwarebury. Anything bigger and they're useless.

Well, despite what I said about Leofgeat just now, I didn't really mind him and quickly gave him to understand that I wouldn't show him up in front of His Lordship, the Earl and Justiciary of Essex. So off I went, flapping my wings rapidly in a great display of panic while Leofgeat kicked off from the leather glove and took after me. We raced off over the lower meadow (centuries later the A1(M) runs straight through it – as I'm sure you know) and then north to Hawkhead Hill accompanied by howls and jeers from the ridiculous assembly of dominant bipeds below. Into the trees we flew and landed together on the snagged stump of an old oak. Here I tipped off Leofgeat regarding some dunnocks I'd seen earlier in the Saxon hedges yonder. Off he went and I flew back around Hawkhead Hill and south to where de Mandeville sat propped up on his saddle waiting for the return of his hawk. I made sure to position myself between His Lordship and the sun as I approached and landed on the tree he waited beneath with a great sound of flapping and the *tick-tick* that Leofgeat makes. As he looked up at me, his hand shading his eyes, I ceremoniously stuck my black arse out over the edge of the bough and shat in his face.

I'd hated de Mandeville for years; his father and grandfather (another Geoffrey) too. When G. de M. senior arrived with William the Bastard in 1066, he took to throwing his weight around for his boss and as a reward was handed large tracts of land along the scarp and elsewhere. He could ride all the way between Enfield and South Mimms solely on lands he owned. It was all moats, vineyards and fine mounts for his like in those days. I hated his wine-stained garlic-laced tongue, the wet farts he made as he ravished the meadow girls. Rights of pannage and estovers were withdrawn from his tenantry; fishponds were filled at Fenny Slade and Holy Hill; everything was misery and the animals died in droves in the forest. His grandson – old shit-face – was even worse, and deserved what he got.

There are the shimmering mornings of early summer, when the land is lit yellow-green and waits in a hazed silence before the madness of cars erupts. There are sea-black winter nights when the air punches its way in from the Atlantic with a deep booming, a reminder of human fragility lost to you in your heated Range Rovers. There is the sadness of autumns when ancient farms finally fail, replaced by filling stations, or when estate houses such as Mrs Brightwen's are given over to tinny housing estates (whatever you do, don't tell her what I've just said: it would kill her).

I love Mrs Brightwen and bring her horse chestnut burs;

I bring her bleached rabbit bones and small bits of rusted metal. I *could* bring her Boudicca's jewelled dagger but refrain: some things are best left alone. Mrs Brightwen always accepts these gifts happily and places them in the felt-lined glass cases where she keeps her collection of Egyptian beetles and Amazonian millipedes. She has a remarkable knack of communicating with, and taming, animals – particularly birds – and her friend Jack (a jackdaw, wouldn't you guess?) is a favourite of hers. I like Jack too and always take the time to listen to his tales of woe. The jackdaws are being eased out of London Town and – just like us rooks – are hated by farmers too. Wait until the ringneck parakeets arrive I think; then you'll see avian revenge writ large. I resent the way my tribe too have been displaced by the dominant bipeds: the rookeries of the Inns of Court; the seven hundred trees of Kensington Gardens: all gone!

Once, down at Roxeth (you'll know it as South Harrow) I saw that lanky anthropocentrist and careerist Thomas à Becket taking a secretive and drunken piss in the communal pond. Disgusted, I 'walked out', so to speak, fast-forwarding timewise past the arrival of the Harrow Urban District Council's gasworks to that ill-omened point in time when the gasometers were replaced in turn by a branch of Tesco *moderne*. I plucked the liver from a grey squirrel roadkilled in the supermarket car-park and carried it to the top of that London plane growing next to the brutalist concrete public convenience erected circa 1972 (you know the one I mean). As I tore at the bloodied flesh I thought of 'Saint Thomas' and of what had been, what was to come. Men of his type were essentially power brokers, claiming a god-given insight into the nature of time in order to justify bludgeoning their way to estates and precious stones and power. It is hard to warrant that multitudes walked tracks along scarp-lands somewhat similar to the one I habitually inhabit in order to visit his jewel-encrusted shrine. Loathsome though he was, I almost have more regard for fat King Henry, despite the ordinances he issued against us rooks. A serial killer if ever there was one, he at least had the honesty to recognise his ambitions were entirely self-serving.

Roxeth was a sort of Crow Capital in the days before the railway (Roxeth is Old English for 'where the rooks drink', as I'm sure you know), a place where we roosted during the winter months, where we spent our days picking over the scruggy flats. After the electric railway arrived in the early 1930s houses began to spring up everywhere along with schools, libraries and health clinics. The rivers and marshes running down from Harrow-on-the-Hill through Roxeth and on towards Ruislip and Northolt were drained. Embankments were built and sewage farms commissioned on our ancient lands. Thus you lot arrived like a bad dream with your vapours and noises, your plastic bags and shopping trolleys. Something needed to be done and I took it upon myself as a kind of tribal elder to organise things: Oxhey Woods, just north of Scarp towards Watford seemed a good place to shift to. I had dealings with the wintering wood pigeons that used the same place and we reached an agree-ment. During the day the pigeons would use the wood – I'm sure you've seen them ascending in great numbers from the trees to circle around for a while before landing again. Come the evening my crew would use it for our babble. It was a sad day we left Roxeth, as we had been there thousands of years. It had to be done, though; even as we gathered on the marshes and prepared to head north, pipes were being buried, new roads laid. It is a quick flick from burghers to burger-bars, from Homes Fit for Heroes to heroin dealers: why would we want to stay? The time had come to leave and we ascended with a massed *kaa-kaa-kaa-kaa-kaa* and flew in a great black cloud northwards across Harrow-on-the-Hill, Greenhill and Pinner Hill to our new roost. We made quite an impression, our flight being commented upon in that week's edition of the *Middlesex Gazette*. I noted in passing that my old friend Daphne du Maurier was visiting her nephew William at Harrow School that day. I oft-times visited the du Mauriers over in Hampstead, playing my clown role for the family in order to rub up against some literary types. I stayed with my rooks a few days only; I'm a loner at heart and besides, the loss of Roxeth, and memories of Mrs Brightwen – long dead by then – weighed heavily on me. I became depressed, wondering where it would end. There were tangible human tensions in the air in the 1930s. I experienced them as dark whorls drilling through to the heart of the declining woodlands and old hedges, seeking to convert the old stone and tussock world into human currency. I left Oxhey one cold November morning; I needed to be alone.

'Merops the Bachelor', Mrs Brightwen named me in her book *Quiet Hours with Nature*. And it's true – I was and always will be a bachelor. Sex doesn't have the same status for us birds as it seems to have for you dominant bipeds, with all your penetration stuff, your sticky warm-bloodied intimacies. Besides, one thing I've learnt again and again is that to love mortals when you live full-planetary time as I do, is to court more pain than any mortal could imagine. To give you some examples of what time can do: I have seen the Haberdashers Girls lying naked and wild as anemones with tattooed Hertfordshire mechanics in the woods and then next thing they are greying and toothless conservatives; I saw Tony Blackburn's youthful smooth-skinned visage sag after three decades living off Barnet Lane; I saw the glory that was Graham Hill mangled in plane wreckage on Arkley golf course. Worst of all, every autumn I see the myriad crane flies desperately attempting to work their way up sun-warmed walls and concrete posts, their legs dangling behind them and wings torn off as the world leaves them behind and no one cares, though they should. Why add to this eternal fading and loss; why breed more death than there already is?

As I mentioned earlier, Mrs Brightwen made friends with a gentleman named William Henry Hudson, an Argentinean American and lover of birds, and together they founded the Selborne Society, named after a book, *The Natural History and Antiquities of Selborne, in the County of Southampton*, by the Reverend Gilbert White. I'd met White back in the 1780s and have always fondly imagined that it was I he depicted in those sections of the book devoted to the rook. Mrs Brightwen and Hudson bought a small wood down at Perivale and sealed it off from human interference as a reserve for birds and small mammals (but of course, you know that). I used to visit the Perivale Wood regularly in the 1950s, flying due south from Stanmore to Harrow and then following the little Coston's Brook down to Greenford Parva. The wood is just to the left by Horsendon Hill. Your books will tell you that this patch of woodland with its fine sessile oaks is a residue of 'The Ancient Forest of Middlesex', but I happen to know that it was, in fact, a timber plantation laid in 1536. It is a fabulous place and much appreciated by the dunnocks, titmice and finches of that area. Unfortunately, sometime in the mid-1980s, a group of ringneck parakeets escaped from a transhipment depot at Heathrow and made their way south to the Thames and along to the Gardens at Kew. They bred and now their numerous offspring have taken over much of the land to Scarp's south including Perivale Wood. All day the parakeets swoop in and out of the trees with a vulgar *whee-whee* and other manners alien to the natives but one must be tolerant, I suppose. Viewed from the perspective of planetary time we are all immigrants.

Later on Mrs Brightwen met Sir Montagu Sharpe, a magistrate from Hanwell Parish, down in the south-west of Middlesex, who awakened her to the shape of the land in their region, its rivers, geology and supposed history. Sharpe fancied himself as an antiquarian; he saw shapes and structures everywhere in his landscape. Throughout his life he remained convinced that the mother churches of Middlesex were aligned along a grid-like template formed by the boundaries of Roman administrative areas. Now, I knew this was all rot, having been around in those days, but enjoyed sitting there perched on the mantelpiece in Mrs Brightwen's day room listening to this curiously lively minded administrator sounding forth, his voice assured and confident as it boomed through aromatic clouds of Short Coloured Cutty. I speak human, as do certain fish, but never made a sound to counter Mr Sharpe's theories. Not only would it have shocked the pair of them but, believe me, the truth is overrated; I know because I have seen it. Mr Sharpe was destined for great things: he ended his days as Chairman of Middlesex County Council and – bless him – founded the Royal Society for the Protection of Birds.

Most people who see me nowadays think I'm a carrion crow. Either that or they think the carrion crows are rooks. They really have no idea! My true kin are now way out in the sticks, preferring to avoid human habitations in so far as this is possible. Incidentally, this is the first time in the long history we have shared with humans that we have made ourselves scarce. I don't know why this is exactly but I think we all sense something deathly about you these days, something you refuse to acknowledge, an unexamined aspect of yourselves which lingers around you and is beginning to rot and stink.

I'm not only a bachelor but also, like all good rooks, a thief. Back in 1974 I stole 'TV personality' Anne Aston's gold and diamond engagement ring from a hairdresser's in Mill Hill. I spotted her wearing it at a garden party in Arkley Lane. I watched from a cypress as she blathered in her muu-muu while absent-mindedly rotating the ring on her finger. I knew her face from scraps of paper – back issues of *TV Times* – dumped in stacks by the derelict King George V playing fields where I slept those days. She was best known for loading the crossbow on a popular TV quiz show. *The Golden Shot*? Who needs it? Certainly not the rooks; golden rings are more our thing. Anyway, I overheard her saying she was booked for hairstyling and pedicure the next day down at Mill Hill and quickly made my plan. That night I followed her back to her home at the White House on Hyver Hall Road – way up on Scarp, that place! – flapping my frazzled wings wearily above the central divide of Barnet Way as I chugged behind her white Mercedes 230SL.

I must add here that I was surprised and delighted to see where Ms Aston lived. Purely by coincidence I had, at one point several years earlier, been friends with the film-stills photographer Fred Daniels, who'd had the White House built for him back in the 1930s. Daniels worked for the Amalgamated Film Studios at Borehamwood, and his job often took him over to Hollywood, where he saw houses built by Frank Lloyd Wright. Falling in love with the style he hired the architect D.E. Harrington to design something similar for him, the house to be built on a site specially selected for its fine views. The White House was the result. I was introduced to Daniels by avant-garde dancer Margaret Morris, who I first met at the headquarters of the Bureau of Cosmovitalist Principles at Lawrence Weaver House in Leatherhead in 1932. Margaret took me up to the White House one weekend for a photo session. The

National Portrait Gallery has a fine print of Margaret and me taken beneath a tree on Witching Hill, just to the south of the White House. I'm reaching across her chin and playing with a necklace of Baltic amber she particularly favoured. When she died I took it and hid it in a crack in the brickwork of an inspection chamber for the East Middlesex Drainage Scheme just by that stream that runs down from West Enfield to the Salmon Brook at World's End. I think you took a photo of the spot a year or so back.

I spent the night perched on the roof of Jane Drew's High Acre (1960). The next morning I heard Ms Aston's car start up outside the White House. In order to stay ahead of her I decided to head directly south of Scarp and through Target Wood and Moat Mount – where John Child had his dentures blown all over his little park-keeper's hut back in 1941. I crossed the brace of once-pretty streamlets that surface in Mill Hill and flow west before disappearing into concrete tunnels below the Barnet Way (they resurface on the Mill Hill golf course and run down between the old Great and Small Burr Fields to the lake at Stoney Wood, as you know). I passed the junction of Barnet Way and Courtlands Avenue where in 1997 Alex Hart, a Luton Town FC supporter, was sent flying after he walked drunkenly into the traffic and connected with a Ferrari travelling way over the speed limit from Shenley to Brent Cross. I glided over the spot where you unknowingly squashed a small beetle in 2003 on one of your little jaunts. By now Anne Aston's car had wound its way onto the arterial road and was catching up with me fast. However, it was easy for me to stay just ahead of her given the morning traffic flow at the junction with the Watford Way (I note that your transport authorities insist on calling this Apex Corner once more. I find this intriguing as the name went out of usage at one point in the 1950s, being replaced with the moniker 'Northway Circus'; hence, I presume, the bas-relief of performing seals on a block of flats close by) and watched as she eventually turned right at Mill Hill Circus onto The Broadway. She parked outside the post-office and entered the My Fair Lady salon.

When Mr Kurland shooed me away twenty minutes later – 'get out of here you filthy vermin'(!) – I had Anne Aston's ring in my beak. She'd been so busy jabbering away to Mr Kurland's assistant and pedicurist Edyta Sikora that she failed to notice my nabbing the ring from the side table where she'd placed it together with her car keys, driving gloves and diary. (I need to add here that after Mr Kurland's death in 1978, I checked the skip full of shop fittings left outside the now derelict My Fair Lady salon. Of particular interest to me was a journal kept by Mr Kurland in 1974, written out in a 1960s Caravan Club of Great Britain logbook. It made for fascinating reading and I would be happy to hand it over to you some time, should you care to annotate it.)

I hid the ring under some rotting leaves in the hollow of an ancient oak on Clay Lane, just by some remains of the old tramps' colony, the one that was broken up after that murder back in the 1930s (I'm sure you know the place I mean). Why I did this, I don't know. I just like shiny things. Last time I looked, just after your millennium, the ring was still there.

Mrs Brightwen contracted cancer and died on a May morning

in 1906. I made arrangements for her favourite cuckoo to call out from a small turkey oak growing close to her bedroom window just before she faded into union with Scarp. She died, opiated and happy, listening to her last cuckoo of spring. Within days the house was emptied out, the animals dispersed to collectors or killed humanely, the beetle and butterfly collections given to the Natural History Museum. Mr Odell went on in later years to become chairman of the Stanmore Parish Council. Over the succeeding years I used to visit him once in a while, sitting on his white gate as he left for work or – after he retired – for the allotment he kept up by Grim's Dyke. I don't think he recognised me despite his insisting on greeting me by my old name. He probably thought I was another rook altogether and used that name in memory of the Merops he knew in the great days of The Grove. Later on the house became a laboratory for GEC Avionics and then for Marconi Space & Defence Systems. I passed that way recently, tracking the uplands as I used to do. The house is now gone, the grounds largely filled with new housing and extensive car parks. It broke my heart to see it, even if I knew it was coming. However, many of the exotic trees remain and, looking around in the rhododendrons close to the swampy spring-pond, I found the old Grotto, the seashells still set in its domed ceiling, the sense of those I once knew still lingering in its chamber.

6

EDGWAREBURY

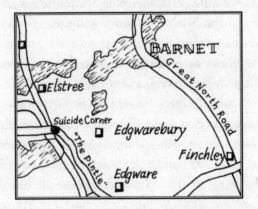

THE ROYAL NATIONAL ORTHOPAEDIC Hospital stands on Roman Watling Street, which runs uphill from Edgware towards Brockley Hill in parallel with the A41 Edgware Way. Looked at on any map dating from the Edgware Way's completion in the 1920s, these two major roads form the shape of a blood-engorged pintle, its ejaculatory duct tantalisingly close to where the source of the Tykes Water spurts out into the hospital grounds.

The land between the two roads – barely a quarter of a mile apart – could reasonably be expected to be one of those 'dead' zones within which no one would choose to live, but in fact contains the hamlet of Newlands at its southern end. This little cluster of private houses is accessed via a footpath at Newlands Corner known as Pipers Green Lane. The path drills through blobs of secondary woodland, crossing the suggestion of a stream in a damp low-lying patch before hitting Newlands. After passing through the exclusive micro-suburb the path comes out onto Watling Street at a good third of that road's way to the crest of the hill.

Edgware Way can be shadowed in its uphill progress by walking northwards through Edgware Way Rough, a tussocky residue of once-rural land just to the east. As I walk the gravel track paralleling the road, I enter a deep and steep-sided bottom at the base of which flows a stream that has its source high above, close to Brockley Grange Farm. The Edgware Way climbs ever higher along a spur until only a suggestion of the cars zipping southwards, in engine noise or glimpse of car roof, remains. The low-lying gully into which I'm now walking was the projected route of a London Transport electric railway that was supposed to connect Edgware with Bushey, with intermediate stations at Brockley Hill and Aldenham. The line would run below Brockley Hill via a deep-bore tunnel, the entrance to which is supposedly hidden in dense brakes of hawthorn somewhere far below the Sulloniacis Pastures – named from their proximity to the site of Sulloniacae, a Roman town or way station that once stood by the side of Watling Street. Back at the base of the hill – opposite Newlands Corner – are the ruins of the brick viaduct built to carry the railway over the Edgwarebury Brook.

This whole swathe of land is a sad place, especially if visited on long summer evenings when the late flowers – the square-stemmed marsh thistles by the stream, the flaccid ragwort and taut teasels growing by the stumps of the railway arches – have been uprooted and replaced by metal posts strung with white tape demarking the pitches for the car-boot sales to be held there the next day. Hidden in the banks of blackthorn and elder tree are pre-moulded concrete cable stanchions placed to serve the rail route, the plans for which did not survive the Second World War.

As I head north through Edgware Way Rough I cross a concrete track. Its left-hand arm ends abruptly a few yards on, at a bank of discarded tractor tyres. Beyond this – on the far side of the Edgware Way, which has sliced it in two – the track continues towards Newlands, passing an impromptu car wash staffed by chain-smoking Albanians. Loneliness always descends as I enter this land of severed or simply uncompleted routes, of weeds, pylons and oxidised tin cans.

To the right, the track leads towards the bleak open uplands of Edgwarebury and Bury Farm. It cuts across sun-scorched fields and past artificial lakes dense at summer's end with water plantain and purple loosestrife. There is brown clayey soil spread across the track in places – it builds up on my boots until the weight of it swings my foot forward as I walk – and rosettes of sow thistle everywhere. As the sound of the busy road junction at Newlands Corner recedes I shift into something new, something unexpected.

Everywhere I find scatterings of pigeon feathers and chunks

of bloody meat on the dry ploughed soil. Linnets flap softly as they fret in the hedges – there are murderers abroad. Red-eyed green-bottles bustle on the feathered remnants, the still-meaty sternums of the dead birds. As I stand over the corpses, the plough-lines curving away draw my eye uphill to a small spinney, the likely roost of the ancient speckled killer: soar sparhawk.

The first time I came this way was in the late summer of 2001, during a period of hospitalisation at Edgware. Tiring of the telly in the day room, the patients' self-piteous talk unravelling like the smoke from the endless cigarettes they sucked on, I escaped for a few hours and walked northwards until I came to the edge of town, a final few yards taking me past a crumbling 1930s shopping parade to this wasteland, these pylons. Somehow I found myself on this broad concrete track, by this rubbish tip and the stream clogged with black binliners. It was here that I stopped and took stock of my predicament. The unmapped landscape I inhabited internally found its exact image in the clutter weed growing at the base of the pylon nearby, in the quietly ticking ant-hills and scraps of fleece caught on the barbed-wire fences. There was the same absence of human proximity – only birds could hear me chattering to myself. As I sat and smoked, watching the mandible motorway a half-mile off dragging never-ending streams of living steel into the city's jaws, my solitude was transmuted into love of this place. The dense mats of sheep's sorrel wobbled at my feet as a sudden blast of air carried me over the city to the dark hills of the North Downs and further off, towards the ocean.

Revitalised and newly militant, I turned and went back to

the hospital. The next day I discharged myself. A week or so later I undertook a three-day walk from my home in Childs Hill to Hertford via St Albans and Dunstable, doubling back through Welwyn and Essendon. En route I travelled through Sir Francis Bacon's old estate at Gorhambury. It was here I found a maroon notebook lying by the side of a B road early one morning and was prompted to begin writing, trying to track the complex interactions between the mind and landscape.

As I climb Scarp's southern face, passing a snagged tree and near-bald pastures scattered with purple and green docks, the hills at Harrow and Perivale come into view. The blue gasometer at Southall Junction; the green slopes of Sunnyhill Park in Hendon; the red-roofed dome of Wakeman's Hill, Kingsbury: these are the cardinal points. And packed between these and Scarp are the human multitudes, their dynastic interweavings too complex to map. Our privileged modernity is as nothing in the face of the onslaught of clouds and air, the globules of sunlight sliding across the land's surface and eating whole postcodes at will. Time moils and folds in on itself under this dancing light. The car, bought, lovingly polished and rocked by sex in a Brent Cross car park 1987 is now scrap, the engine stuffed with grasses, a home for field mice. Your lips, the smell of your hair, the earring you left in my bedroom by accident, which I hung on the tube frame of my 1960s shelf unit as a trophy: they surface to my memory like bones rising in a field.

Streams and ditches run through pipes beneath the chipped and cracked concrete track. These conflux to form the Edgwarebury Brook, which joins the Dean's Brook (a tributary

of the river Brent) at Brookside Avenue in Edgware, after crossing below the Watford by-pass. It is difficult to overestimate
the importance of these watercourses to fox, insect or bird in
the parched summer. Once, just up by Bury Farm, I found the
shrunken dried-out husk of a fox wedged high in a hedge of
blackthorn. One of its hind legs had become trapped in a crux
of blackthorn and the animal had died there. The fox's skin
was a parchment wrapped loosely about a bleached bundle of
bones on which was inscribed a life's journey from heathery
spring through dry-ditch summer to hen-house autumn and
motorway winter. I looked closely at its teeth, pointed and
yellow beneath the curled-over upper lip, and imagined its slow
agony under the sun. Just yards away a narrow ditch carried
an inch or so of water. I was reminded of another dead fox
seen in a disused factory near Trumpers Way in Ealing a couple
of years earlier. There was the same snarling challenge to *my*
skin-wrapped reality bubble. The dead fox lifted me out of the
sunlit day and the concerns of the human world into an open
field of possibilities.

The fate of foxes seems bound up with this exposed swathe
of horse country. Up ahead is Bury Farm, a seventeenth-
century farmhouse with a double-gabled and jettied upper-
floor. Nowadays it is a riding school. All day the cars cruise
up and down the approach road, dropping kids off for their
lessons. I often stop when passing and stare into the farmyard,
wondering how best to manipulate someone on the staff into
sneaking me inside so I can take some photos of the interior.
Usually I'm seen off with a severe look by one of the female

riding instructors and go loping away in my raincoat feeling curiously guilty. However, these long glances of mine have fixed the position of a tree standing behind the farm firmly in my mind and I was able to compare this with the one visible in a photograph I have of the farm entrance taken in 1947. This particular picture is of a hunt leaving the farm. And there they all are: the moustachioed ex-officers – recently demilitarised – in their jodhpurs and their scarlet jackets; the stupid-looking dogs straining for the chase; the whippers-in in their checked caps, sullen and obedient. And there is the same tree, standing black and patient behind the old farmhouse, destined to watch decades of car journeys sweeping past on the yet-to-be-built M1 motorway extension that now cuts along the ridge just north of the farm.

Edgwarebury Farm, demolished in 1965, stood a hundred yards or so further up the track towards the motorway. The farmhouse was replaced by a curious Swiss chalet-like building. Close by are small cottage-type dwellings and a derelict Portakabin standing in a yard strewn with clinkers. I escaped from rain once by entering the cabin through a hole knocked into the plywood door. The place had that damp burnt smell often found in deserted dwellings. A rancid mattress surrounded by cider bottles and fag packets told of its unofficial use by other wanderers. The kitchen was a mess of splintered chipboard in the middle of which lay an overturned sink. I stood in the kitchen doorway and smoked while the rain rattled against the roof. The sound of water dripping to the linoleum floor intensified the cosiness I felt. Finally the rain stopped and a burst of sunlight diffused through the scratch marks on the Perspex windowpanes. I decided I'd had enough and left. Outside, a woman wearing a headscarf led a coated horse towards the farmyard. We averted our eyes from one another as we passed. The scoured ditches gurgled and my breath – still laced with nicotine – misted my glasses. The February landscape was hissing with damp and I thought of the curled foxes, warm in their hidey-holes somewhere deep in the angled land.

Middlesex & Hertfordshire Notes and Queries, Vol. III (1897) includes a communication from a Mrs Brightwen of Stanmore regarding a petition dated 1808 lent to her by a neighbour, in which the 'Noblemen, Gentlemen and Farmers of the neighbourhoods of Harrow, Pinner, Watford and Stanmore' objected most strongly to the activities of the Berkeley Hunt. Their objection rested not on any perceived cruelty to foxes but on damage to property, the value of land so close to London far exceeding that on the distant moors and heaths. One of the signatories was Mr Sam Ridge, who owned Edgwarebury Farm. As if in revenge, the following year the Berkeley Hunt rampaged across Mr Ridge's property and his newly laid drainage whelms (tree trunks halved vertically and inverted to provide a secure watercourse) were kicked and broken as the fox was chased, chased until its final terror froze in the air, hanging like some cold, shrill bird-cry for ever.

Yet I love it here, high above the city's trammelled process. I recall coming down off the hills from Edgwarebury one dark November evening in 2006 and catching a bus back to Childs Hill from the electrically lit by-pass. As I entered the warm security of the bus and glanced at the passengers sitting and reading their *Evening Standard*s, I had a feeling of having returned from some transtemporal substratum of the manifest world, as if I had visited the Underlands, those deep, throbbing hive-centres where the energies that underpin the disparate phenomena of the stockbroker belt are generated.

I sat, and as rain specked the window I passed into the land-scape. I was saplings and bushes. I was ditches of black water and prefab barns made from asbestos and breezeblock stand-ing in winter fields 1954. I was wind-whacked days with shirts drying on washing lines at Deacon Farm 1962. There was a mewling of gulls and air carried in from the Atlantic, laden with memories of trawlers and tankers. As the bus crossed the North Circular this heightened awareness of the land and its memories began to fade and by the time I alighted at Childs Hill my consciousness had reverted back to its usual state. Forgetting all I had seen, I pulled my collar up in the cold air and scurried off to Moby Dick's for chicken and chips.

Edgwarebury Lane – a road that parallels the pintle – runs directly from the Watford by-pass uphill to Bury Farm. This is a good route to take if you want to gauge the magnitude of the slope forming Scarp's southern edge. The climb is along a wide suburban street lined with large brick houses built in the 1930s. These are true detached villas, each one supposedly distinct in detail yet curiously faceless when taken as part of the mass. As I ascend I look back and watch the rooftops of Edgware begin-ning to appear.

A darkness hangs over Edgwarebury Lane: the murderer

Daniel Raven lived here, in a large cornerhouse on the right-and side as you head upwards. He killed his parents-in-law at their home in Ashcombe Gardens – just across the Watford by-pass – one night in October 1949, battering them to death with a heavy TV aerial. Raven was arrested on suspicion and a search of his house revealed bloodstained clothes smouldering in the boiler furnace. Cross Gate, the road leading off Edgwarebury Lane from Raven's house, links to a series of concentrically arranged crescents, the middle of which is Franklyn Gardens. It was here, in April 1938, that Jean Mitchell, a supervisor at Golders Green post office, strangled her seventy-nine-year-old mother. Raven was hanged for his crime; Jean Mitchell was more fortunate, ending up incarcerated for an indefinite period under the Mental Health Act.

Behind the houses on the opposite side of Edgwarebury Lane is Edgwarebury Park, through which its namesake brook runs before disappearing into emergent woodland near Edgware Rough. The park contains relics of the old field systems, traceable in lines of tall sessile oaks and fastigiated hornbeam. A large ornamental scent garden provides views down onto the by-pass.

Down along the by-pass some of the old villas are being demolished to make way for luxury flats. Stacks of yellowed documents and biscuit tins of photographs are probably going up in smoke even as I look. I wish I could take them by the hand, the people who once lived in these red-roofed houses 1949. Now they are mere names inscribed on gravestones in overgrown suburban cemeteries. The delicately edged gardens, nurtured for decades, have been robbed by cancer of the attention they needed and ossify into parking spaces outside care homes. It was all thrust aside, this new life 1960, in a rush of sports panels and game shows; a moment's tenderness given over to Jimmy Hill, Sunday afternoons 1976.

Eventually, after a slight dip, Edgwarebury Lane breaks out into the wide expanse of pasture land and rural rides that form the Edgwarebury uplands. It comes as a shock, this shift from parked cars and front gardens to old hedgerows and fields. As I keep an eye out for the 4x4s that come up from behind, I move ahead along the treelined lane. Down to the left, across the fields, is the valley of the Edgwarebury Brook and further off, on Brockley Hill, a row of street lamps pokes above the treeline, demarcating the route of Edgware Way. Walking ahead there are periodic old oaks and a pair of solitary lodge houses. I once saw nuthatches descending one of the trees here, climbing downwards head-first as is their habit; a lady I met walking her dog insisted the birds were tree-creepers, but I knew she was wrong.

Further on, after the farm and the Portakabin, the Swiss chalet and the cottages, the path climbs sharply to cross the M1 through an area once known as Edgwarebury Common. Up until some time in the 1970s a London Underground train carriage, propped on bricks, served as home here for a family named Crawford. It was listed in the local directories as Railway Cottage. Up and over the route climbs, towards Scarp's spine on Barnet Lane but that is another story. A turn to the left just north of the motorway, over a tube-steel gate and across farmland attached to the Edgwarebury Hotel, leads to a steeply sloped band of fields divided from each other by barbed-wire fences. Ahead runs the A5 to Elstree, Radlett and St Albans and below, the motorway slices through Scarp in a ha-ha that renders it invisible and unheard – only the slim curved lamp posts and a grey gantry indicate its presence – before it curves north towards Hemel Hempstead. Once again the pigeons, reduced to torn feather mops lie scattered on the fresh-turned clay. I count twenty dead birds spread over a fifty-yard radius from where I stand. The narrow band of woodland along the edge of the motorway cutting is particularly bloody, the corpses mangled, heads ripped off, stomachs pierced and one bird hanging from the crook of a tree, its neck elongated and twisted, its silvery-straw eyes fixed on the uncaring traffic.

Later I'm back at the small lodge houses, by the nuthatch tree, looking eastwards along a muddy, broad footpath winding through dense trees and high hedge. This is the aptly named Clay Lane, an ancient route to Edgware. Following this, and taking pleasure in the red campion, the wild roses and the adder's meat, I stumble through alternating seasons of snow and heat and the unrecorded histories of ant colonies, deaths of rabbits, furious wasps trapped in spider webs. I cross over the dome of land at the lane's heart to emerge onto a flat table of heath a good quarter-mile broad, at the far end of which runs the M1 motorway and a long straight stretch of railway. Pylons straddle the landscape, the fizzing from the power lines interweaving with the sound of lorries and cars filtering through the wet trees. Everywhere there is a sense of loss, of time slipping away, and an equal sense of arrival. As I walk I call out two names, waiting for a pair of ragged figures to jump out from behind the fat oaks and close in on me, cudgels in their hands. Sweating, I place my face against a cool mossy concrete lintel marking the footpath's edge and phase out.

*

It was a Monday night in early June 1931. As yet there was no motorway to Birmingham, no Jumbos whistling overhead towards distant Stansted; only the railway and some sidings given over to the dumping of refuse defaced the otherwise rural air of the place. Smoke curled away from the burning refuse tips and faded into the tall oaks lining Clay Lane half a mile away. There were flames licking at the base of the railway embankment along which trains periodically crawled before halting to dump rubbish. The fire had been burning for years.

An itinerant labourer named Michael McGlade left his shack on the edge of Scratchwood and approached the flames, endeavouring to obtain a light for his pipe. Suddenly McGlade stopped and stared: protruding from the smouldering refuse was the unmistakable form of a charred human arm. Glade dropped his pipe and ran off down Clay Lane to seek help.

This arrived rapidly: two police officers happened to be riding along the recently completed Watford by-pass Road on one of S Division's brand-new motorcycle combinations. They had been inquiring into a series of burglaries at nearby Moat Mount Golf Course and were about to question some gypsies on a local encampment when McGlade hailed them. The officers dismounted and followed the tramp up the narrow old country lane. The shift from the machined carriageways of the arterial road to the mud track climbing between dense hedges must have seemed like travelling back in time fifty years. Yet what these dutiful officers, fresh from their high-speed dash along the by-pass, were about to see was like something out of the Middle Ages.

McGlade took them to the spot, where a quick glance confirmed the man had been correct. One of the officers headed back down to the by-pass to get support while his colleague and McGlade sat and smoked, guarding the body.

Chief Constable Ashley, Superintendent Savage and Divisional Inspectors Bennett and Andrews from S Division joined them shortly after. A true local 'bobby', Detective Sergeant Pickett, who was to prove a great help in the subsequent inquiry, accompanied these highly experienced officers.

Close examination of the find revealed it to be the body of a well-built man partially hidden in the stack of smouldering detritus, his head pointing towards Elstree. Part of the trunk of the body and left forearm were burned. Upon removal of the corpse, it was found that the right forearm and both feet were burnt off. A piece of charred sackcloth was wrapped about the head.

The body was removed to the mortuary at Hendon Town

Hall and the officers involved began to speculate on how the deceased had ended up in such a remote place. The initial view was that the as-yet-unnamed man was the victim of an accident. However, the possibility of foul play was not ruled out.

The following day the eminent pathologist Sir Bernard Spilsbury examined the body. He concluded that the cause of death was fracturing of the skull and injuries to the brain. The man's jaw was also fractured and there was a large wound to the chest. His features were beyond recognition, with the exception of traces of a sandy-coloured moustache. On one arm was tattooed a red heart pierced with an arrow. Spilsbury reckoned the man to have been dead about thirty-six to forty-eight hours. In Spilsbury's opinion, the injuries resulted from repeated blows with a heavy instrument. The police now had a murder inquiry on their hands.

DS Pickett attended the post-mortem and expressed the opinion the deceased may have been one of the itinerant men who slept out in huts and sheds in the vicinity of Clay Lane. In his view, they were 'a quarrelsome kind' of folk. Pickett was later to be credited with possessing a 'local knowledge of the district, and persons of the class to which the dead man belonged'.

Discreet approaches were made towards some of the more trustworthy members of the Clay Lane tramp community and this rapidly began to pay dividends. A homeless labourer agreed to visit the mortuary to assist the police in identifying the murder victim. He recognised the body from its build and the remains of the moustache as that of a fellow tramp named Herbert Ayres, known to his friends as 'Pigsticker'. The man had been missing from his hut on Clay Lane since the previous Sunday.

Events now moved swiftly. A travelling labourer named John Armstrong contacted the police and made a statement in which he said that he had spent the previous Saturday night drinking in Edgware and had slept at Clay Lane in a hut shared by two members of the tramp community. Their names were Oliver Newman and William Shelley, though their peers knew them as Tiggy and Essex Moosh respectively. Armstrong divulged certain facts concerning Newman and Shelley that rendered it necessary for the police to arrest the two men on suspicion of murder.

Armstrong's statement gives us a compelling portrait of the two suspects:

Moosh is aged about fifty. He's five foot seven or eight. Medium build, full-faced. Clean-shaven, with a very dark complexion. Hair, black. Black eyes. A woman is tattooed on his arm. He is dressed in striped cords, dark blue tweed jacket and waistcoat and a light trilby hat. Tiggy is about sixty. Five foot four. Thick build, round face, clean-shaven, pointed nose. Hair brown, with a sallow complexion. He wears a light-grey coat and light trilby hat.

A team of officers was assembled for the purpose of making the arrest, consisting of those mentioned earlier in this account, together with PC Seabrook. When this was done, the group headed off to achieve their aim.

DI Bennett describes the circumstances leading up to the arrest:

> *Although it was dark, I accompanied the three officers* [Seabrook, Pickett, and Andrews] *to the vicinity of where Moosh and Tiggy's hut was. Sgt. Pickett knew that these men had three ferocious dogs, and so soon as any person approached within fifty yards of the hut the dogs began to bark. However, we were able, by discreet movement around the bushes surrounding this hut, to ascertain that both men were there.*
>
> *Clay Lane has not been used for many years. It is covered with thick bushes and trees on the hedges and also in the road. The grass has grown four or five feet. Knowing that these two men were desperate characters, and that one false move would raise the alarm, and therefore result in both men getting away in the darkness, or in any struggle that might ensue in effecting an arrest, I deemed it advisable to remain there with the officers until dawn.*
>
> *I posted officers at various points to prevent either man escaping across the fields, and with Inspector Andrews and one or two other officers, placed myself in hiding at the entrance to Clay Lane, on the Watford by-pass.*

The officers waited through the night, until, at 7.15 am they saw Shelley approaching along Clay Lane. DI Bennett promptly stepped out from his hiding place and challenged him. He said: 'I am a police officer. You answer to the description of a man named Moosh.'

'That's right,' Shelley replied.

Bennett then said: 'I am making enquiries into the death of a man known to you as Pigsticker, who was found dead at Scratchwood Sidings on Monday June 1st.'

Shelley's heart must have sunk as he found himself surrounded by police officers and the game clearly up. 'I don't know who you mean,' he said. 'I know nothing about it.'

Shelley was cautioned and removed to Edgware police station where Newman, who had followed down the lane a little later, eventually joined him. The Edgware Police Station in Whitchurch Lane was still under construction and, as a result, some of the cells were being used for administrative purposes. Nevertheless space was found for the two prisoners, who were relieved of their jackets, which were taken away to be examined for evidence.

The arrests having been made, the officers then took the opportunity to visit the tramps' little colony of shacks and sheds. Here they found a hefty stick, which had clearly been cut from a nearby bush. It was stained with blood and adhering to it were some hairs the colour of the dead man's moustache. Bloodstained grass was found in a hedge were it had been hurriedly thrown after being cut from the ground around the shacks. Worst of all was a large axe discovered hidden beneath the planks forming the floor of one of the dwellings. Close by was a bucket containing bloody water.

When he returned to the police station, Inspector Bennett was told that Shelley wanted to speak to him. 'I will tell you something of what happened,' Shelley said and upon being cautioned he made a statement in which he admitted to having murdered Herbert Ayres with the assistance of Newman. According to the prisoner, he and Newman had come into conflict with Ayres over the latter repeatedly stealing tea and sugar from his – Shelley's – shack. Neither he nor Newman had intended to kill Ayres. Later Shelley told DS Pickett, 'If I could have had my way you would never have had us. I wanted to put him on the line and let the train hit him, but Tiggy would not have this. Still, he has got all he has been asking for for a long time.'

At 7.20 that night Newman and Shelley were charged with the wilful murder of Ayres, to which they both replied 'I don't understand.' They appeared the following day at the Hendon Petty Sessions. According to newspaper reports neither had shaved for a few days. They were described in the *Hendon Times* as 'shabbily dressed, of the roadster type', the report drawing attention to the fact the two men were without their jackets. After hearing evidence from Inspector Bennett the pair was remanded in custody to appear at the same court a week later. The accused applied for defence fees under the Poor Prisoner's Defence Act.

In the meantime the police continued to take statements from various members of the Clay Lane colony. Despite Shelley's protestations concerning their lack of intention to kill Ayres, the police had managed to build up a considerable amount of evidence that suggested otherwise. They felt they now had enough to successfully prosecute Newman and Shelley for the capital offence. The main thrust of the prosecution rested on the statement made by John Armstrong. This contained an account of the murder as witnessed by somebody who was actually present at the time, the details of which completely undermined the story given to the police by the accused. Armstrong had stayed at Clay Lane on the night of the murder and had bedded down in Newman's shack some time before that man, Shelley or Ayres had returned from Edgware. Upon retiring, Armstrong had successfully dozed off but was wakened by the sound of raised voices outside the shack. Shortly afterwards he heard a number of loud thuds and a man kept shouting 'Oh dear.' The voice was that of Ayres. Looking out into the moonlit lane Armstrong saw the forms of two men whom he recognised as Newman and Shelley, and one was striking Ayres with a 'blunderbust', a sort of wooden cudgel. After that things had been quiet for about twenty minutes. Hearing another thud, Armstrong had peered out of the shack again and saw an axe being dropped into a pail of water and the two tramps lifting what looked like a body before carrying it off in the direction of the railway sidings.

Understandably, John Armstrong had been terrified and he resolved to make himself scarce at the first opportunity. He lay quite still lest the two killers became aware he had witnessed the murder and the following morning made his excuses before packing his things and leaving. As he was setting off Moosh had approached him and said: 'Jordie, if anyone asks you about Pigsticker . . .' to which he replied: 'Yes, I know all about it. Mum's the word.' After reading a report of the murder in the press he had decided to go to the police and make his statement.

Richard Saunders, who lived in an old van on Edgwarebury

Lane, made a statement in which he described having seen the accused in The Boot public house in Edgware on the night of the murder. According to Saunders he had asked them why they were looking 'so savage' to which Tiggy had replied: 'There will be something up if anyone comes "mooshing" around our place.' Saunders was worried the tramps were referring to him but was assured that they were talking about 'the Pigsticker'. Later that night he had heard a man repeatedly crying 'Oh! Oh!'

Fred Cozens, who lived in a shed on Edgwarebury Lane, knew the prisoners. He told the police he had been sitting on a bus with Ayres at Edgware Station that night, when Tiggy and Moosh had looked inside. Tiggy undid his coat and Cozens saw what he thought was an axe in his belt. Tiggy had nodded in the direction of Ayres and then the two men went away.

The accused appeared again the following Wednesday before a special sitting of the Hendon magistrates. J.S. Hogg presided and Charles Wallace presented the prosecution's case. J.A. Morley defended Shelley and J.M. Lickfold appeared for Newman.

The case came to trial at the Old Bailey on Wednesday 24 June before Mr Justice Swift. The outcome was a foregone conclusion as both defendants had effectively incriminated themselves through their statements. It is difficult not to feel a measure of sympathy for the two ageing rogues; both attempted to convince the jury the murder was justified because Ayres had repeatedly stolen their tea and sugar and their bacon. One feels, upon reading the court transcripts, that they possessed only a rudimentary understanding of their predicament and of the machinations of the law.

The following afternoon Shelley and Newman were found guilty of murder. On being sentenced to hang Shelley remarked to the judge 'Thank you, Sir. It ought to have been done years ago.' The condemned pair was led chuckling to the cells.

An appeal against the sentences was lodged but was subsequently refused. Tiggy and Moosh were hanged in a dual execution at Pentonville prison on 5 August 1931.

*

I came out onto a wooden podium separated from the rest of the courtroom by sheets of thick Perspex topped with steel meshing. The dock looked out onto a baffling scene, one that I instinctively knew spelt danger for me. If I'd expected the courtroom to reflect some sort of grandeur or sense of gravitas given its connection to the Crown, I was disappointed. There was none of the fine oak panelling, the oil paintings, heavy velvet curtains and brass fittings I'd imagined.

In fact the courtroom trod a fine line between utility and intimidation. A small disgusted-looking woman wearing flyaway glasses, a black robe draped over her narrow shoulders, stood on the green carpeted floor before me. To my left, set notably higher than the rest of the court, was a panelled dais on which sat three stern and seemingly remote individuals whom I took to be the magistrates. The middle of the three was a large-faced and grey-haired man with a broad, wrinkled brow. He exuded an air of wealth and self-satisfaction, of expensive aftershave and the creak of polished shoes, and had something of the lion in his strong, handsome features. His seat was set higher than his two colleagues', indicating his authority; this was undeniably his show. To his right a younger – and clearly less important – man with a thin, elongated and smoothly shaved face stared across at me. Perched to the left of the chief magistrate was a middle-aged woman who bore more than a passing resemblance to my local MP Margaret Thatcher. She glanced at me momentarily and then down at some papers on the desk in front of her, idly fingering the pearls hanging across her beige mohair cardigan. Behind them was a board upon which were inscribed in gold lettering the names and dates of the presiding chairmen of the court dating back to the late 1890s. The courtroom was a distillation of all the immensity and continuity of the county council.

I swallowed hard and wiped my sweating palms on my jeans. This is where I get it, I thought as I stared into the lion's mouth.

'Number seven: Nicholas Papa . . . Detritus,' the lady with the flyaway glasses announced, struggling over a typed list in her hand.

I looked about me, at the grate mounted in the ceiling behind the magistrates, the tiered and deserted benches in their own enclosure off to the side by a large door. Another set of benches marked 'Press' was also empty.

'Sit down Mr . . . Papa . . . Derrida,' the chief magistrate said.

'Sit down,' the copper, who had followed me into the dock,

repeated, jabbing me in the hip, as if somehow I was not allowed to simply comply but had to be cajoled into conforming to the dictates of authority.

An attractive woman with shiny brown hair and long eyelashes sitting in a row of seats in front of me stood up. I felt a surge of hope. She's got to be on my side, I thought.

'Sir, the case for the prosecution is . . .' she began, and my heart dropped. The idea that so resplendent a creature, someone so in contrast to everything else I had experienced over the last few hours, should be arguing for those who wanted me punished horrified me and further enforced the idea I had that my position was hopeless. She then outlined the details of my offences and my arrest. As she came to the point where I'd handed myself in I noticed that somehow the pitch and phrasing of her description of my voluntary arrest suggested that I was a danger to society, someone to be treated in a harsh and unforgiving manner, as if, if I'd been less of a liability, I would've attempted to avoid detection.

'We are concerned that Mr Papa . . . Doppler may reoffend unless he's held in custody. We are therefore asking for a period in remand,' the brown-haired woman finished and took her seat again.

I noticed that the three magistrates were all staring at me intently. I swallowed nervously as David stood up, his flared suit looking ridiculously ostentatious in this harsh place.

'There's nothing much to add at this stage in the proceedings, except that my client has requested legal aid and that we will not be applying for bail right now.'

Not applying for bail? Who said? I tried to get David's attention as he sat again, waving my hand at him through the Perspex sheeting.

The copper jabbed me in the hip again. 'Keep still,' he whispered.

The chief magistrate conferred with his colleagues, their murmurings barely audible through the screen that separated me from the rest of the court. The Margaret Thatcher look-alike glanced at me with a look of distaste and then back at the other two magistrates.

Finally the chief magistrate looked across at me from his raised position and spoke.

'Mr Papa . . . de . . . Retro, this is a serious charge and, as you heard, the prosecution have concerns about the likelihood of you reoffending. You will therefore be remanded in custody for five days for psychiatric reports, to appear before this court on Tuesday next.'

With these words the clerk and the magistrates dismissed me from their minds and started shuffling papers about on their desk. I saw David lean forward and say something to the brown-haired woman in front of him and they both laughed. He was conferring with the enemy. The copper took my arm and pulled me round and began to lead me to the stairway down to the cells. No bail! What then? Surely I wasn't actually going to go to jail? But I was; that much was clear.

'Hang on a minute,' I shouted, twisting free of the copper's arm, 'what about bail?'

Margaret Thatcher and the chief magistrate looked up, their

faces severe, as if my outburst was beyond anything that could be imagined in their courtroom, though surely such eruptions occurred almost on a daily basis.

'Take him down, please, constable,' the clerk commanded, speaking for the magistrates.

'Come on, lad. No trouble,' the copper said.

'No. I want bail,' I shouted. 'They told me I would get bail.'

'C'mon, no trouble,' the copper insisted, raising his voice slightly, but I wasn't having it.

'No, I want bail, you cunts. You told me I'd get bail.'

This did it. Everybody, the magistrates, court officials, the duty cops, solicitors and their clerks stared at me in disgust. David stood up and shook his head urgently from side to side, attempting to silence me.

'I said no trouble,' my copper rasped and grabbed my right elbow, yanking it forward and up as he placed a hand under my right shoulder and lifted. The door leading to the cells opened quickly and the turnkey emerged, gasping for breath, and gripped my other arm.

'Get down there,' the turnkey hissed.

My eyes watering, panic swimming through me, I passed through the stern portal. I was on my way.

We descended the cement steps into the strip-lit grimness, now more than a mere way station on my privileged tour of the underworld. The grimy windows, the dull green walls saturated with decades of crown-sanctioned stasis, claimed me. In tears, I was pushed into my cell, the turnkey slamming the door shut behind me. A small steel flap set into the door opened.

'Your solicitor's coming down to see you. Now don't make trouble,' I heard him say. And then the flap slammed shut again.

Breathing hard, I looked around the cold cell, threw myself onto the bench and pulled my coat across my waist and chest. I lay listening to the rain hissing against the ground outside, my mind in a fury. How dare they treat me like this! Slowly I calmed down. It was warm under the coat and opening my fag packet I counted twelve smokes – enough to last me a few hours. I wondered whether I would get some more when I arrived at the prison. I began to speculate on what it would be like inside and this gave me a curious comfort. After all, I was definitely on some strange kind of adventure, a journey to lands barely imaginable. Who knew, the experience might imbue me with certain characteristics I felt were lacking in myself, a degree of hardened masculinity, or a flinty philosophical dogmatism, a geezer's stolid knowledge of what was what in this world. It might make me attractive to women or provide material for a seventeen-page modernist poem I was already composing. I might emerge from prison a saturnine and moody character, someone driven by a deep-rooted impulse to walk alone over the hills and tramp through the edges of satellite towns leaving nary a trace. Perhaps I would eventually end up the subject of a feature on BBC *Nationwide*, a man of interest to the arty crowd in Belsize Park. Arriving fresh from my appearance on some late-night culture show on BBC 2 I would plonk down the expensive bottle of wine on a smoked glass coffee table and look around at the array of ringlet-haired glories gazing at me in interest, their long floral dresses sweeping the pile carpeting in some plush pad with a balcony overlooking Hampstead Heath.

An hour passed and the mood faded. I stared emptily about me. I ran my eyes up the line formed by the meeting of walls in the corner of the cell and then across the ceiling, taking in again the lamp nested in its flat Perspex shield. Then I looked over at the window, the dim winter light making its own contribution to the misery of my predicament. Growing bored, I fixed my eyes on the floor tile in the corner of the cell nearest the door. I moved my eyes on to the tile beside it and then the one after that. Each shift of my eyes was accompanied by a sharp jet of breath discharged through my nostrils. I worked tile-by-tile along the row immediately in front of the cell door and then, with a little hop, moved onto the next row, which I began to work through in the opposite direction. Out in the corridor there was the sound of continual opening and closing of doors, feet echoing back and forth. Later I heard someone whistling and keys rattling on a chain.

I lay down and dozed for a moment, entering a sunlit landscape somewhere out in the green belt. I arrive back from my unspecified job in the city, my dark blue Lotus Europa snorting as it crunches across the gravel drive. I enter the white modernist house, visible from a distance to meet once again with those arched eyebrows and the togetherness over fondue and Mateus Rosé.

The key sounded in the lock and my door flew open.

'Solicitor to see you,' the turnkey barked.

David walked in and sat down on the bench next to me. I sat up and gazed about, looking for my glasses and cigarettes.

'I thought I was gonna get bail,' I said.

'Look, will you just fuck off about bail,' David snapped. 'The magistrates, in their wisdom, have decided to have you remanded for reports. You'll probably get bail next time you appear.'

'So I've got to spend five days in prison, yes? Well, that's just fucking great. And what am I supposed to do in the meantime? Just sit there in some hole, waiting for my dad to get off his arse and show up in court, if he can be bothered?'

'Look, stay calm and we'll get you out next Tuesday, I promise. I'll make sure your dad knows where you are,' David said.

There was nothing else to say, so after looking about the cell for a moment, David rose and left, the turnkey peering triumphantly into the cell before slamming the door shut.

I stood smoking and waiting, poised on the edge of something vast and beyond any experience I'd ever had. Already my friends, my dad and brother, the bedroom in which I slept, read and smoked my Capstans, had receded, somehow becoming miniaturised – a set of discrete entities itemised, bagged and labelled 'past life'. I was on the cusp of the real adventure, a journey fraught with trepidation. Contemplating the approaching darkness I laughed – perhaps hysterically – and waited, listening to the rain as it sizzled against the concrete of the yard outside. Finally the turnkey came and unlocked me.

This was in the days before Securicor and other private companies looked after the transfer of prisoners and so I fell under the custody of a couple of prison officers – the first I had ever seen, both far older than the policemen I had been cuffed to earlier and with coarser uniforms – who handcuffed me and led me up the concrete steps and out into the courtyard to where a long blue wagon with darkened windows waited, purring and rattling.

'Into the sweat wagon, sunshine,' one of my guards said and – having learned my first article of prison nomenclature – I hauled myself through the door and into the long narrow interior.

Inside, the sweat wagon stank of cigarettes. As we walked down the long galley, voices called from behind the doors of the cubicles that lined either side asking for lights for fags or demanding to know whether the wagon was going to the Scrubs or Brixton first. We reached an open cubicle near the rear of the bus and I was told to enter. It was so small inside that I had no choice but to sit down on the hardened plastic seat. The window – its rounded corners and heavy rubberised sealing suggestive of the porthole of an aircraft – was broken by strips of some inlaid material that sliced up the view of the outside world. As the door closed on me the men in the other cubicles shouted to one another and began to harass the screws regarding my arrival.

'What's with the four-eyes, chief?' someone demanded while the person in the cubicle immediately behind me spat out the single word 'nonce' and gave the partition wall a hard kick, the energy of which transmitted through to my seat causing a painful ringing in my back. A slam of the wagon door announced our departure and as the engine started up the whole vehicle began to judder and quake.

I squinted through my little porthole as we reversed out onto Archway Road. The half-familiar street seemed displaced, the pavements and parked cars now located in another world. All the people passing by would carry on with their life-dance without me.

Suddenly I was hungry for the roads and houses that sped past as we turned off towards Highgate. As we hit the high street a wave of anger rose in me; the small delicatessens, their windows packed with salami and French cheeses, the cafés filled with scarfed and perfumed women, a second-hand bookshop frequented by Trotskyite intellectuals: these all spoke of a world I would never access – not now. I was bound elsewhere and wondered why not even one of the faces I saw as we passed looked up at the long blue vehicle hissing and whirring towards the road to Hampstead.

This was doubly sad because recently Highgate had become the very nexus of my twin aspirations of (sexual) love and bohemia. Situated as it was on the margins of my imprinted world, Highgate served as a bridge between the dullness of my home suburb and the lights of the swinging city. Somewhere in my adolescent mind I confused it with a Pacific port – probably San Francisco – as depicted in various novels I'd read or films I'd seen while straining for a life where something actually happened. My most recent visit, the previous summer, had been a case in point: one hot afternoon I'd wandered up there after taking the tube from Woodside Park to East Finchley. To my mind there was a sort of democratic sexiness about the place. The whiteness of Highpoint flats, nested on their cliff-top; the Archway Road, thundering like a freeway below; the steep streets with their expansive views to the south and east; these all suggested sun-soaked skies, art galleries, perhaps even jazz clubs. Surely the Pacific Ocean lapped against these Northern Heights.

Of course, beautiful people inhabit beautiful towns. That day, while probing about off the Archway Road, I saw a young girl exit a house and descend the steps onto the pavement before walking towards me. How splendid she seemed, a muse designed to stimulate the songs of experience I so yearned to compose. With her petite yet somehow knowing middle-class face, the smattering of dark freckles spattered across her soft shoulders, her long patchwork skirt, her wool scarf and tumbling hair, I could imagine her taking a tram up the hill, visiting her poet lover, and opening a curved American fridge to remove a bottle of white wine. This was a world I longed to inhabit.

Later we ran past Hampstead Heath, which I remembered from visits there with my mother in about 1965–66. With its frost-encrusted oaks and beeches and its sodden brambles, it seemed to speak an older language than the civil streets. Something welled up from the twisted dead stems and reached across to me – the possibility of a safe-haven, an eternal counter-poise to the madness within and without. When we reached Hampstead the sweat wagon edged in behind the local magistrates' court where we picked up several more prisoners. Then we headed south, through sooty Camden with its semaphore signals giving their *sieg heil* from the iron railway bridge spanning Chalk Farm Road and on to Tottenham Court Road. We visited Bow Street and Horseferry Road Magistrates and then crossed the Thames into a winding of narrow streets somewhere around Lambeth. This was the city I'd long dreamed of and now I was seeing it.

7

WELHAM GREEN

I T IS 20 JUNE 1975, five months before my arrest, and I erupt through the front door of my house in Woodside Park. As the door slams behind me I hear my dad shouting through the living-room window: I'm a good for nothing, a bloody farmer (I think that's what he said); I'm ill in the head and a waste of time; he kissed my bottom when I was a baby when in fact he should've strangled me at birth. Well, fuck him: I'm off and out, propelled by my fury past the Kalamazoo offices with their mosaic pillars, the scented cornershops and the humourless rationality of the police station at Whetstone. I'm heading north, always north and not caring where I end up. All I know is that I must escape this city, the relentless chatter, the pressure to succeed.

I'll sleep in ditches or potting sheds. I'll claw mangle-wurzels from the obdurate earth and suck on sugar beets behind aluminium silos. I'll grow hairy and mythic in the stockbroker belt. I imagine the waiting fields, the fine houses throwing their shaded light on tangled woods. I yearn for love in the cool darkness of ancient barns.

I walk down Barnet High Street unnoticed by the weekday shoppers and look back from the church down into the seething, fly-infested ditch of the Thames Valley. The city is spread out below, its denizens squashed into flared jeans, striped tank-tops and embroidered denim jackets. Everyone I know is psyching themselves up for tomorrow's big concert at Wembley Stadium: Elton John; the Beach Boys; the Eagles; and Rufus – whoever the hell they are! The music I grew up with and loved seems to no longer be mine. Two days back I saw D—— tapping her foot to 'Takin' It Easy' in the sixth form block. Then that smooth shit Tony approached her smiling, a copy of *Captain Fantastic* tucked under his arm.

I walk through Barnet and pass the obelisk celebrating the Battle of Barnet in 1471. I move on and the road becomes a straight highway to somewhere else, somewhere altogether different. There is a flattened rabbit on the south-bound side of the road and, after a mile or so, fields drop down steeply to the right. I look across the dip to the blueness of trees, white office-blocks glinting miles off and pylons following the crest-line. These draw me into their current and I'm flashed through the region at the speed of light. I am a lineman for the county, a flitting presence in this wavering ocean of sunlit wheat and barley. I can see into your rooms, savour your lives.

At some point soon I should pass through the veil and people will be different, the styles more old-fashioned, relations purer, less governed by avarice. The cars will be squarer, and uniformly black, hair less modish. The strain of string quartets, not the Incredible String Band will sound from windows, the smell of rabbit stew or jugged hare waft from porches. But, as the miles slip by, the usual bright green Capris and metallic blue Vauxhalls zoom by in either direction, self-assured city faces staring out at me as they pass.

I come to Potters Bar, a place I have heard of but never visited. A tall office block, Canada House, towers over the road and the paper shops, I notice, sell the Kit-Kats and Mars Bars, Number 10 cigarettes and boxes of Callard & Bowser's butterscotch I see on sale in London. I cross the road to a record shop and look through its window. There's curly haired Leo Sayer, gesticulating like an idiot in his clown costume; the haggard Easter Island faces of the Stones gaze at me from some sumptuous tropical paradise; Bowie in his checked shirt, lounges forward out of his album cover, smoke twirling from his cigarette. It is the same old assembly of fools. I look away in despair and see a bus pulling out of the depot opposite. It's a number 134 heading for Friern Barnet – a mere half-hour's distance on foot from my home. All the miles walked in this merciless heat; all the glimpses of hope, anticipation of expanding vistas amount to precisely nothing: I'm still trapped in the shared world. There is no escape here – it could be Archway or Camden Town for the difference it makes.

There's only one solution. I have to go deeper, carry myself further, and on an impulse turn right down a side street and within minutes escape the last of the bungalows. I'm on a narrow lane with trees on either side. Off to the right I can see across the valley I looked down into on the road from Barnet earlier on. A flock of wood pigeons explodes from the left and a horse-trailer hauled by a muddy Land Rover overtakes me. The driver, a healthy-looking red-faced man dressed in dungarees smiles as he passes. I think I can hear sheep somewhere close by and my pace quickens: this feels more like altogether somewhere else. The lane curves to the left and drops down to a small stream that emerges from a desolate pocket of woodland. The sun is at its zenith now and I have to plan where I will sleep tonight. I've no toothbrush and I'm swimming in my own sweat and besides, I haven't had a bath in weeks. No farmer will take me in, his smiling wife provide me with milk and eggs. I grow thirsty and my eyes water in the light dazzling from the surface of the road.

A car roars by, the sound of *Dark Side of the Moon* jangling through its open window. I pass a pile of horse manure in the dead centre of the road. A small pig-like deer disappears into a clump of bushes on the edge of a field, its rump rising and falling as it seeks to escape me. Then a helicopter appears over from the east and strikes off towards the south. Flowers I cannot name grow everywhere along the wayside and a used condom hangs from the branch of a sapling by a stile. Am I still within London's gravitational force-field or not? I can't decide.

And neither do I particularly care. I'm feeling sick and exhausted, my mouth is dry and I feel weak with hunger. I need to rest and up ahead I see a farmhouse and, further off, a brick railway viaduct crossing a broad verdant valley. Dare I drink from the stream that undoubtedly runs beneath the viaduct? Or will a particularly beneficent farmer bring me a slopping pail of cold water from his well?

I look over the white gate. There is a tractor parked by the side of a henhouse and a sign crudely painted on a sheet of hardboard: 'Colesdale Farm. Egg's and Fresh Tomato's'. Behind the farmhouse is an old wooden barn with sliding doors. It looks cool inside and I am overwhelmed by a desire for sleep. I climb the gate and cross the yard, my ears open for the 'Oi!' I expect to hear at any moment, or the bark of some ferocious dog. But no one notices my presence and nervously I enter the darkness of the barn. I climb the piled bales of hay and peer through a gap in the planking onto a sun-scorched orchard behind the house. I hear a train surging across the viaduct a half mile away. I wonder where it's heading and imagine the passengers, envying them their escape from London.

I wake hours later and looking through the gap again I see the shadows of the apple trees have lengthened. I wish someone were here to share this with me. I think of my mother, sick in her council flat down in south London. I'm miles from home, in a place I have never visited before and – bad news all round – I have carried myself with me.

It is now January 2006 and I catch the bus from Childs Hill to North Finchley, change for High Barnet and, alighting by the church, charge off along the Great North Road bound for Potters Bar and beyond. I'm due to have lunch with a friend in Welham Green, some miles to the north, and hurry on with no time to write notes or consult my map. Not that I need to – these ways are well known to me now.

There is an alleyway that runs north from Potters Bar Station alongside the railway track and through a straggling industrial estate. I turn left onto Cranbourne Road, where the buses wait before making their return journeys to wherever and there are no houses, no pretty gardens or conservatories flashing in the winter sunlight. This is the service quarter of the town, where warehouses and council depots lurk, out of sight of the more salubrious drives and crescents of Potters Bar. Across the road is Furzefield Wood, where the urban district council placed its sewage farm after the town expanded in the 1930s. It was closed down when the West Hertfordshire Main Drainage Scheme came into commission after the Second World War but the trunk sewers still run below the ground here, in parallel with the Potters Bar Brook. Hidden in the grass are broad concrete plates – access points to the sewer – and a slightly fetid air lingers in this otherwise attractive dog-walking countryside. Off to the left is sixteenth-century Mymms Hall, high on its mound and, further on a ford crossing the Mymms Hall Brook.

The A1(M) runs on an embankment ahead, and, in front of it, the dead road of the old Barnet by-pass shadows it, clearly overwhelmed by its brash usurper. It's a strange presence, this 1930s through-route rendered obsolete so soon after its completion. Despite its still being maintained in order to serve local traffic, the by-pass's broad carriageways serve a mere fraction of the traffic they were designed for. The result is unsettling, suggestive perhaps of a landscape which has been depopulated by a virulent epidemic. I follow the road northward towards North Mimms. On the left I can see the high ground at Hawkshead Wood and over my shoulder lies South Mimms and the extended barren heights of Ridge with its austere stone church and myxomatised rabbits.

The coming spring will see fan-leaved cow parsnips and the spliced petals of pink campion growing along the stream's edge. Somewhere over the motorway lies the motte-and-bailey of Geoffrey de Mandeville's castle, largely torn up for the extraction of chalk. A kestrel hangs steady over the thick tangle of blackthorn, just days away from flowering, and, a mile further on, the Mymms Hall Brook has had its embankment strengthened, the V-nicked length of concrete flood wall reminding me of a medieval bridge.

I hurry on, so as not to be late for my appointment, leaving the roadside to climb Dixons Hill to Welham Green. I walk down Dellsome Lane and into a café and she's there, sitting at the very same table where we first ate together years back. I unpack my rucksack, spreading maps and notebooks out on the tablecloth. As fried eggs on toast and warming cups of tea arrive, we sit and smoke. And she tells me all about it:

*

I will place my neck on the railway track by Skimpans Farm. I will feel the irons sing and then boil, hear the whir of the approaching wheels, the rising drilling roar of the turbo-charged locomotive as it closes in and finally engulfs me. Then my head will bounce across the clinkers and roll down into the wormwood and the poppy flowers. I will rest by cable conduits and become food for ant and rat, a hatchery for maggot of flesh fly. I will sink unnoticed into the county, this river-addled land of memories and defeats.

But the breeze will still smooth circles in the long grass by Skimpans Farm. The ant colony by the electric fence will continue with its work, the queens crawling to the tops of grass stems before opening their wings and launching into the heavy July air. The stream will keep to its business too, blurting and popping as it pulses through the corrugated plastic pipe, carrying pockets of air with it. The horses will stand and piss languidly as they stare up at the raised railway track where the train sounded its urgent warning and I screamed as I faced my imminent voluntary departure.

Then the driver of the Cambridge train will radio ahead from near Skimpans Farm. Then my friends will miss me and set out, worried in their cars, searching the lanes until they find my 1960s lady's bike leaning by the dock-infested nitrate-rich horse enclosure. Then the Hertfordshire constabulary will seal off the footpath with plastic tape as my headless remains are hauled by guy-rope to the embankment's edge and carried off, blanket-covered, by ambulance. Then my bloated puckered visage will stare fixedly from its dusty nest of viaticals before shrinking down to a leathery black husk. Then I will be mentioned in the *Potters Bar Times*. Then the memory of Gloria will be frozen, Parnassian, in notebooks and poems. Then I will rest, embedded in the land, my struggle ended.

I lurch across fields of yellow rape from Hawkhead Hill until I reach the low ground at Waters End, a place where streamlets come in from all directions before disappearing into swallow holes. It is an exact correlate to my own desire, this comfrey ridden sump sucking the land's very life-giver down into its chalky maw. I too desire to draw it all to myself, to take it all in. I too desire to combine with the very earth and be identical with its totality. I wander through the tangles of yellow-coned bittersweet, the stands of nippled sow thistle, and then climb towards Dixons Hill, leaving the path halfway up to cut across stubbled crops, the better to get the view over to the Elstree promontory as it bulges north towards the lost village of Titburst, or – when I swivel on my ankles – the BBC aerials by Old Kentish Lane. I survey this province of mine and prepare my farewells. I am Gloria Geddes, Queen of the PAMS, a clan of psilocybin-saturated pantheists now dispersed to prisons, psychiatric units and – worst of all – the straight life.

As I stare down on these supinated lands, these fields and copses I once fondly imagined were my own, I think yet again of the arched inquiring eyebrows, the aquiline face and thick dark gypsy hair of Raggadagga, Grand Ipsissimus of the order of the PAMS and my very own snarling, biting lover. Raggadagga decided two years back to desert the order he founded and head westwards to Pinner, to work with *her*, Miss

Cosmovitalist Bureau, with her spotless, white lab coat, her coterie of clean-living and chinless yoga teachers and rebirth specialists pranayaming it up in their commercially made isolation tanks and orgone accumulators. Raggadagga has seemingly acquired a taste for this type of antiseptic New-Ageism with its money-love, its polished crystals and cheap cosmic bric-a-brac straight out of some two-bit god's suburban gift shop.

I spot a bird skull sticking up out of the clay and, yanking it free, I place it to my brow. I stare at this little gift of the earth through crossed eyes, trying to fuse with its thin translucent universe. Nothing happens and I sling it angrily into the crucifix of wild treacle poking out of the stony ground nearby. Next, I bend my knees to kiss the sphagnum moss matting the damp earth where a field ditch feeding the Mymms Hall Brook runs through a belt of thistle and willow herb. I taste its clean cool wetness, feel it tickling the edge of my pouting lips. I tune my ears to the trickling of the water and wait to cross over the event horizon.

But it's no good. I merely feel ridiculous kneeling there in my paisley cagoule, my canvas shoes soaking up the turgid water. The obdurate earth gives me nothing. Raggadagga has withdrawn his sanction, emptied out my landscape and sucked the vitality and meaning from stone and plant behind him in the slipstream of his withdrawal. It is too much (and has been for a good few days now, I admit) and today I can take no more. Tears come and I begin to howl and screech in my animal pain. My fury drives me uphill to the margins of Welham Green and I enter Dellsome Lane, which passes as our high street, unashamedly blubbering at the injustice of it all. I cry inconsolably outside the Dellsome Foodstore, despite the efforts of kindly old Mrs Lewis to calm me. I try for the sugar fix at the baker's but the sight of all those trays of coconut and chocolate cakes – substitutes for what is missing, what is gone – merely intensifies the loneliness. I'm even indifferent (probably for the first time in months) to the filling station attendant's smiles and winks. Raggadagga has left me – I must face the fact – taking my stomach, my appetite for either food or love-making with him, and there is really nothing else I can do other than return to my sparse bungalow, to my Nick Drake and Moody Blues LPs, or end it once and for all today.

I sit on the bench opposite the plaque celebrating Vincenzo Lunardi's balloon flight in 1784 and reading it for the thousandth time I finally understand why he unceremoniously dumped his pet cat and dog on the locals after landing here and then promptly set sail again. Simply put, he saw what was on offer at Welham Green and, like Raggadagga, couldn't wait to get away.

One sopping wet day in the late 1980s, I came across a scruffy-looking man busily gibbering to himself on the pavement outside the Silhouette dry-cleaners. I stopped to listen to this frizz-haired and unshaven odd-ball with his stained canvas rucksack and worn walking boots and when I overheard him muttering about something he called his county consciousness, I immediately recognised him as a prime candidate for the PAMS. He was clearly the worse for wear and so I treated him to a cheese sandwich at Simmons Coffee Shop where I broached the subject of his joining us.

Sadly, the prospect held no joy for him. He had his own angle on things he told me, his own version of why the received world is nothing more than a mass hallucination. Reaching into his rucksack he pulled out a rain-soaked stack of notebooks and maps and, sweeping aside the salt pot and ash tray, spread them out across the Formica tabletop. Staring out at me through glasses spattered with the residue left by the acid rain, he spoke of the geological structure of the region, of his home in an obscure suburb of London. He reckoned that walking 'against the structural grain of the civitas', as he put it, led to a 'thin enlightenment, a release into the things found scattered on the soil'. He then launched into a spiel about plant consciousness, fusion with bollards and motorway memories, stuff I understood and knew.

Anyway, amongst other things he informed me that Welham Green is perched on the high ground dividing the valley of the river Colne from that of the Lea. The idea of that excited me, making me feel as if I were at the very hub of the county's water systems. After seeing him off on his long walk southwards back to London I rushed home and put on some Vaughan Williams, his *Fantasia on a Theme by Thomas Tallis* providing a back-drop to my musings on the language of the earth, its shapes, colours and changes. I felt inspired.

But today I see this place as nothing more than a mean little cluster of houses, a tight-lipped pub and a few second-rate shops. It's hard to believe that I once loved Welham Green, happily adopting it as a new home after things fell through at Borehamwood, what with all those drug busts and Dagenham Steve ending up filleted and packed into a cardboard suitcase.

I first clapped eyes on Raggadagga in the summer of 1969 after me and my friend Brenda sneaked off without telling our parents, intending to inveigle our way into the ATV studios at Borehamwood. We wanted to be part of the audience for that week's episode of *The Golden Shot*. There was no joy though. A jobsworth security man turned us away after Brenda rolled her eyes in disgust at his come-on.

After wandering around town for a couple of hours we went into a milk bar and there he was, sitting in the corner, book in hand. I still remember how I caught my breath when I first saw those flashing eyes and the long straggly black hair I was to love for the next four decades. Raggadagga looked up at us as we ordered our coffee and immediately invited us to share his table.

'Ah, will you join me, my little cosmic doves, all flown here from beyond Sirius?' he said, running his eye up and down my mini-skirted body. 'I am Raggadagga, Uncrowned King of Middlesex, habitual dweller of progressive ballrooms and organiser of happenings, street theatrics and occasional riots.'

'So, what do you do for an encore?' Brenda asked, eyeing up this magisterial presence sitting before us in his purple loons, orange T-shirt and fairground scarf.

'That, young lady, is for me to know and for you to find out,' he answered with a conspiratorial wink. 'Anyway, what's your story? First time in Borehamwood?'

'We're down from Luton for the weekend, darling,' I replied, looking him straight in the face. 'We fancied a change for the better.'

'Luton? Hmm. That's in the Midlands or somewhere, isn't it? Have you heard of the Beatles up there yet?'

'You cheeky sod!' Brenda said, grinning. 'Hark at Mr Flashy-Pants here. Shall we go and sit somewhere quieter, Glow?'

Brenda was joking, of course. Both of us were entranced by Mr Raggadagga. We'd never met his like in Luton.

We sat quietly for the next few minutes, sipping our coffee while Raggadagga seemingly put us out of his mind and returned to his book.

I wanted to talk to him a bit more but was frightened that Brenda had annoyed him.

'What's the book then?' I asked, finally getting up the courage to break the silence.

Raggadagga held the cover up for me to read: *Psychedelic Prayers* by Dr Timothy Leary.

'Oh right. Any good?'

'Well, it's OK in its own kind of way, I suppose, but I don't think Leary knows as much as he fancies. For instance, he links the psychedelic experience to each of the senses in turn but doesn't go much beyond that. Now, *I've* worked out a way of redirecting the body's vital energies into objects in order to experience them from within. A kind of non-localised consciousness, I suppose.'

'What are you talking about?' exclaimed Brenda, her eyes wide with alarm. I wanted to ask the same thing.

'LSD.' He emphasised each letter in turn as if these told us all we needed to know.

'LSD? You mean the drug?'

Brenda and I had heard of the stuff, of course. It was part of the London lifestyle we read about in the *News of the Screws* every Sunday. We'd never taken it though; in fact we'd barely even tried alcohol, being fifteen years old.

'LSD is not a drug. It is a sacrament,' Raggadagga answered irritably. 'It opens up the mind to the true nature of reality. Politicians, teachers, television, our parents – they brainwash us into thinking this . . .' and here he gestured to the tables and chairs surrounding us, the counter with its cupcakes on display and the waitress scratching her nose as she gazed out the window '. . . is reality. But it is not. It is a world peopled by robotic sleepwalkers.'

'So what is reality, then?' I said, hoping to annoy him with my challenge.

Raggadagga snorted and looked down his nose at me as if I were some ridiculously stupid creature, unworthy of respect.

'Reality, darling, is something you clearly know nothing about – yet! Still, coming from Luton I don't suppose you know much about anything, do you?'

I wriggled awkwardly in my chair, feeling he'd sussed me out. I was pretty innocent in those days as to the ways of the world.

'Well, come with Mr Raggadagga and I'll show you the true nature of existence.'

He rose from his chair and towered imperiously over us. Then he brushed his hair back behind his ears, picked up his book and put it into his embroidered bag. 'Now is your chance to find out, darlings,' he said, looking back at us as he reached the door. 'All I ask in return is that you pay for my coffee.'

It was then that we noticed he was wearing green cowboy boots with three-inch heels. We burst out laughing. Raggadagga looked mortally offended for a moment and then joined in with us.

Raggadagga turned Brenda and me onto LSD that afternoon. As we walked through the streets of the town, with seagulls circling overhead, he handed us a pill each. I looked down at the neat little pink thing resting innocently in the palm of my hand, excitement welling in my stomach. I felt I was on the threshold of something life-changing, but little did I suspect that the events of that afternoon were to preoccupy me one way or another for the rest of my life.

Raggadagga took us up a side street that led uphill through a housing estate to a long stretch of barren high ground I later knew as Woodcock Hill. It was an astonishing place with views of Borehamwood and beyond. We sat on the grass and knocked back our pills with a mouthful of Fanta. And then it happened. As Brenda twittered on about Scott Walker and *Crossroads* – our usual schoolgirl points of discussion – I began to feel most odd. The bushes and trees around us hardened into a sort of crystalline obstinacy and thrust out stroppily into their three dimensions. Then Brenda's face went the other way and became lopsided, as if made of melting plastic. At one point she twisted her head and left her eyeball behind, suspended in the air above the thistly grass. A sense of horror permeated everything and, feeling scared, I lay down and focused my eyes on a tiny forget-me-not struggling to survive in the twentieth century. My blond locks fanned out before me and tangled with the flower's hairy little stem and I felt connected to it, identical with its striving. All the while Raggadagga ignored us, sitting cross-legged and gazing out over the land below. Finally he started humming to himself and the sound bore down deep inside me, becoming an electric buzz, a primal vibration. I hooked onto it and travelled up through a region of brilliant colours swirling somewhere in myself and then rose into pure atomic light. I disappeared into a silent, still place where change no longer occurred. After an indeterminate time, I heard Raggadagga summoning me back to the earth.

'It's time to join the creatures, darling,' he said. 'Hurry up, they're waiting for you.'

And I did join them, though whether it was inside me or in the actual world I don't know as the distinction between the two was pretty much irrelevant by then. I became a squirming mix of feather and fur, claws and incisors. At one point I thought I was an ageless crow. Then I melted into an ivy-clad wall and became a bright red bloodsucker working its way across the sun-heated brickwork. I became a dovecote and my birds flapped gently in my rafters while the hands of an old clock set in my roof twirled through the years, carrying me out of our time into an uncertain future where the earth was trapped in a glistening electronic mesh and a hideous motorway circled the whole of London. I saw skyscrapers collapsing and smoke-blackened deserts, all-seeing electronic eyes on every corner. I grew scared and Raggadagga hugged me, all the while rambling on about levels of consciousness, energy flows and the true meaning of the Hindu myths.

But I didn't care about any of that stuff. I just wanted him to sleep with me.

And that night he did, in the little room he rented above a record shop on Elstree Way. Brenda – whose trip from all accounts had been nowhere near as eventful as mine – slept on his sofa and I shared his lumpy narrow bed.

On the way back to Luton the next day Brenda told me she thought Raggadagga was an idiot but I'd experienced two things that weekend that stayed with me for years: the possibility of leaving my body and fusing with the world. And sex.

Then it was back home and another week at school. My parents hadn't even noticed I'd been gone, by the way. They thought I'd been up in my bedroom all weekend. I returned to Borehamwood to see Raggadagga every other weekend and we experimented with LSD and what Ragadagga called Tantric sex. He introduced me to his little coterie of fellow travellers: Lady Lucy, a buxom south-coast witch and friend of Hugh Hopper from the Soft Machine; Toby, a speed dealer from Watford, who was so anaemic he seemed to border on transparency; and handsome and rugged Dagenham Steve, who looked like Edward Fox.

When I left school a few weeks later I split from home and moved into a shared house with Raggadagga. It was around this time that he decided to honour my presence in his life by 'getting his act together'. At first I thought this might involve his looking for a job but that just wasn't Raggadagga. Staring at me gravely over the African coffee table scattered with Rizlas and scraps of tobacco that formed the centrepiece of our living room, he announced that he'd decided to form a new religion, a cult based around the use of hallucinogens as an exploratory tool to access deeper levels of consciousness. Its members were to take the name the Psychedelic Ancients of Middle Saxony (or PAMS), their aim being the constructive use of mind alterents – 'more Barclay James Harvest than the Rolling Stones' as Raggadagga put it. As the order's founder, Raggadagga would assume the role of High Priest and have the main say in who could join. We made contact with a bespectacled Middlesex Polytechnic student named Deva who manufactured large quantities of LSD in his bathroom. I got a day job in Woolworths and Raggadagga claimed social security and worked on a book of rituals for the PAMS. Every Saturday night we held court for the various freaks, drop-outs, wizards and dealers who hung out in Borehamwood. We kept a huge pot of vegetable stew on the go in our kitchen and, after eating, we would all lie down on mattresses in the sitting room and blow our minds while listening to LPs by Egg or Kevin Ayers.

The PAMS' rituals focused on using LSD to access what Raggadagga called 'morphogenetic memories', layers of consciousness stored in the human cortex, each corresponding with a stage in mankind's evolution from amoeba to the fine specimen of reason that gave us the atomic bomb, napalm and Engelbert Humperdinck. According to Raggadagga – and I must admit that this sounded plausible to me, especially when high – evolution had unfolded according to a plan, a grand design worked out by a highly advanced being or civilisation somewhere far off in the universe. The human mind contains locked within itself levels of future consciousness which we had to activate to save the race and the planet.

In order to achieve this, he designed a set of rituals that actually resembled those rather sexy adult games one finds at sophisticated parties held in places like Surbiton and Purley that I'd read about in the *News of the Screws*.

Not that I cared. As long as Raggadagga was there, everything was OK. Neither was it all bullshit. The drugs did seem to take me somewhere. I remember one trip where I closed my eyes and pressed my brow to a fist-sized piece of Hertfordshire puddingstone we'd brought back from a day trip to Aldenham a few weeks before. In the darkness of my mind I saw a green geometric pattern shifting and changing and seemingly emanating from the flint-specked stone. I focused on it and travelled up the latticework of light into the groaning, grinding heart of a glacier as it retreated slowly north over aeons, depositing its boulders and gravels onto mounds of dead sea creatures and thick belts of clay as it did so. Then the slow action of wind and rain worked its business, breaking the deposits down into loam. Trees grew up in the soil, eventually covering the landscape, and a bearded, grunting hominid (I thought I recognised him as one of the dealers from the council estate down the road) suddenly emerged out of the undergrowth carrying a large flint which he promptly used to smash in the skull of a rabbit who happened to be grazing nearby. Then a railway line appeared and bungalows popped up out of the ground like mushrooms. Commuters used jet-packs to travel to work and the Prime Minister dressed like Jimi Hendrix. Everything was alive. Everything was changing. I felt I was a conglomerate of different times bound by some biological cement into the identity called 'Me'. It was very profound.

Our little Saturday night sessions became extremely popular with the locals. Groups of bikers came down from Stevenage to join us and occasional members of the TV and film industries clustered around Borehamwood in those days dropped in to see what we were about. Raggadagga loved it, taking on the role of all-purpose Wiseman and Prophet. Such was his ability to project a saintly and spiritual side of himself that he was even consulted unofficially by the local vicar concerning the growing use of cannabis among schoolkids. We thought it was hilarious.

Things changed in the early 1970s though. Slowly we were suffocated by washed-up hippies, soap-dodgers and oafs who had discovered dope, thieves all of them. Our LP collection thinned out week by week and the sessions became heavy and disturbing. Things became especially messy after smack began to appear on the scene. Raggadagga and I managed to avoid it through the rigours of our discipline but Lady Lucy became badly hooked, turning almost overnight from a proud extoller of neolithic goddess-worship into a whining witch, forcibly attached by her addiction to a set of knuckle-headed dealers from Watford and – when they'd finished with her – reduced to hawking her mutton for fivers at the Spider's Web motel.

It was around this time that Dagenham Steve ended up shot and dumped in Aldenham reservoir as the result of a screwed-up deal for speckled blues, and Raggadagga and I decided to quit Borehamwood.

What with all the problems, things had become strained between us and so we set up separate homes, though still remaining lovers. I moved to Welham Green and Raggadagga got a flat just down the road in Darkes Lane, Potters Bar. The heroin mess and the murder had persuaded him that he needed to tighten the rules of membership in the PAMS and further systematise the process whereby we accessed morphogenetic memories. This would involve the use of yoga, hallucinogens and sex. The way he explained it to me was thus:

Yoga, with its numerous postures (or 'asanas') named from animals (the cat, the cobra, the fish, the crab and so on) was clearly a coded recapitulation of man's evolutionary tail, a reprise of his billion-year journey from protozoan algae still manifest in his morphology. Each posture, therefore, keys in with and triggers the morphogenetic memories interlayered in the mind–body loop and corresponding with the creature after which the posture is named. The use of LSD while practising these asanas induces a greater sensitivity to the influx of impressions emanating from our morphogenetic memories. Controlled sexual arousal increases the psychic energy available, which, if directed properly, allows the emergent morphogenetic memory to 'jump' out of the body and into a corresponding life form nearby. We would literally become another creature for a duration to be established experimentally. Obviously, if these energies were not guided, they could do more harm than good.

Raggadagga introduced me to Eric Schofield, a dentist living at Slowmans, an old farmhouse in How Wood near St Albans. Eric was a former member of the Order of Woodcraft Chivalry, a group of radical nature freaks who'd been operative in the New Forest in the 1920s. Eric had lost interest in Woodcraft in the early 1930s after becoming disillusioned with the wilder edge of the order – in particular the worship of Dionysus and the nude sunbathing – and had left to join the Labour Party. Nevertheless, he dug out some of their rituals of induction and initiation – things that Raggadagga felt the PAMS sorely needed in order to avoid the chaos that had been Borehamwood. We established our experimental base in the North Mimms Memorial Hall, a post-war pebble-dashed Nissen hut-type structure which we hired at a reasonable rate. Here we developed a series of procedures designed to project us out of ourselves and into the minds and bodies – the 'experiential field', as Raggadagga called it – of the various flora and fauna that shared our environment with us.

Raggadagga placed discreet ads in *Muther Grumble*, an underground magazine we subscribed to, asking any fellow freaks in our area to try us out and we managed to build up a small but significant following. A guy from Harefield named Tizer (on account of his red hair) signed up to our way of doing things and brought large amounts of home-grown grass with him. Sara Langtry, a glamorous and wealthy young yoga teacher, drove over from Pinner in her silver Mercedes to be with us. There was also a thin gangly academic hippy named Robert who'd fallen foul of the Church of Polytantrism in Chalk Farm after ripping off their sound equipment. We didn't care as it was common knowledge that they'd nicked it from Van Der Graaf Generator in the first place. Finally, a fine specimen called Lokabandhu (also known as Roger) fell in with us after Raggadagga dropped in at a Buddhist ashram in Hertford looking for candidates. Roger and Robert were gay so there were no problems with the sex side of things.

Every Tuesday and Thursday we would meet up with the others at the community centre and Sara would take us through a rigorous yoga session. Then Raggadagga would lecture us on his theories. After checking that the doors of the hall were locked we'd place sheets of cardboard over the windows and, dragging out the rubberised mats used for PT that were stored in a cupboard in the kitchen, we'd get down to business. A red light bulb and Indian music completed the setting. Wriggling and twisting out of our clothes, we'd lock in our frenzied drug-fuelled embraces and aim high, aim to go beyond any previously known state. Sara would match off with Tizer and I'd hunker down with my Raggadagga as usual.

We found that a combination of high doses of magic mushrooms and yohimbe was particularly efficacious. Raggadagga and I picked the mushrooms during the autumn rains from a meadow with a stream running through it adjacent to Elstree aerodrome (the same stream that joins Tykes Water just to the east of Kendal Hall Farm I found later). The yohimbe we ordered from a company in the USA after finding it advertised in a copy of *High Times* picked up at Compendium Books in Camden Town.

The yoga and sex certainly pushed me out of myself, but not in quite the way Raggadagga suggested. Yes, my consciousness was 'non-localised' but as yet there were no fusions with specific animals, plants or objects in the experiential field. Rather, I would take a kind of soul journey through many states and, enthralling though it was, it wasn't what I – or rather Raggadagga – thought of as the real thing. I became woodlands and river valleys. I flowed, an iron-rusted streamlet, into broad alluvial marshlands. I was plant successions and the spoor of animals, sour green berries and clicking insects in late summer grass. Time hung over the murmuring land as I moved on to endings at oceans, at salt spray and feather-clad wildness. When I reported this in our after-session debriefings, Raggadagga seemed annoyed as if I were letting the side down. The others didn't seem to get it either, with the notable exception of Sara, whose beatific and self-righteous post-trip reportage began to irritate me, though it clearly brought pleasure to Raggadagga.

'I was a snail,' Sara would declare breathlessly as she pulled on her skirt at the end of a session. 'I could really feel the snake within,' she'd say, her big eyes ogling Raggadagga's naked torso. You *are* a snake, dear, I'd think, though I managed to hide my annoyance from everybody.

When the summer came we practised out of doors and I began to make progress. Finally, one sticky July day, I 'passed out' properly – it was at Poor Field, a sandy belt of heath land just to the west of the Ruislip Lido near Ducks Hill. We sat on a blanket in a quiet corner away from the dog walkers and ramblers and undressed. After a quick yoga session we ate our sacraments and 'climbed aboard' as we put it. The drugs hit me hard and I strained through a sense of impending death that left me retching and feverish in Raggadagga's arms. I suffered a period of impossible nausea (this was a common experience – we often referred to it as 'passing through the eye of the land') and then surfaced through a sort of mist to find I'd become a hornet clinging to a man's shirt slung carelessly into the grass by a furze bush during a family picnic. I remember well the poise and pulsing power of my body, the red warmth of the visual continuum, the flowers glowing like other-worldly beacons, and the itch of mites slowly dissolving the chitin of my long deadly abdomen. I wound through tapering purple ribbons of pheromone, bound for something ineffable that was hanging suspended like the sun in its power. It was hornet-life itself.

I flew through seasons of hornet-time, gold-flecked days. I nested with my fellows in a hollow tree, feeding larvae with caterpillars, wolf spiders and green-bottles. Waves of light and dark rolled across my senses and – the sun setting further south now – I binged on apples rotting in orchards, the nectar of ivy and the contents of discarded beer-cans. Finally I was crushed to death after I flew drunkenly up a man's trouser leg. Escaping from the hairy darkness in panic I settled for a moment exhausted on the ground. Strange but I could've sworn I recognised the toad-like face of Reginald Maudling, MP for Barnet staring down at me as he raised the rolled copy of *The Times* that killed me.

I came to after what seemed like weeks away to find the others standing over me looking worried. They were all dressed and seemed ready to go.

'I got it!' I shouted joyfully. 'I was a hornet!'

'Really?' Raggadagga sneered. 'Well, I'm very glad for you, because the rest of us have had our trip ruined by your ranting. Do you know you've spent the last half hour slagging off poor Sara here?'

I looked round and saw Sara standing by a clump of furze, a triumphant gleam in her eye.

'But I got it, Raggadagga,' I cried, tears beginning to run down my face.

As the others turned away in disgust Raggadagga threw my clothes over to me. 'Get dressed,' he barked and turned to put his arms round Sara's wasp-like waist.

'Are you all right, darling?' he purred, muzzling her throat with his beak-like nose.

'I'll survive, thanks,' Sara replied.

'I think I'll be off now,' Tizer said awkwardly. 'I'm giving the others a lift. See you Ragga. Bye Sara, bye Gloria.'

As I pulled on my top and reached for my jeans I noticed Raggadagga and Sara were deep in conversation.

Raggadagga turned to me as I stood, dressed at last.

'Look, Gloria, Sara and I need to talk about something important. Do you think you can make your own way home?'

'Sure, Ragga,' I said, feeling stung.

'OK. Well, I'll see you later.'

'Bye, Gloria,' Sara said and to my horror she reached out and shook my hand as if it really were goodbye.

Then they were gone.

I wandered around the lido for an hour or so. The children riding the miniature railway that circled the large artificial lake waved to me as they rushed past and then disappeared into the trees. Like Raggadagga, they were moving beyond me, leaving me to my memories, my crow's-feet and thickening ankles. I climbed up through oaks and hornbeams to Haste Hill and sat on a bench overlooking London's northern suburbs. I could see planes coming in to land at London Airport. A blue gasometer and the swirling hills beyond spoke of distances, of divergences. The huge and incalculable array of sparkling houses and office blocks, of parks and roads spread out below, seemed to groove to its own rhythm, a dithyrambic ecstasy that echoed the event undoubtedly taking place between Raggadagga and Sara even as I sat there. Wiping my eyes, I turned away and made my long way home.

Days later a letter from Raggadagga arrived. He'd decided to dissolve the PAMS and had given up drugs and begun to train as a yoga teacher. Sara had re-mortgaged her house and they were going to set up a 'growth centre' – 'The Bureau of Cosmovitalism' – in Pinner together.

'There's money to be made in this business,' he wrote. 'Sara and I are partners now. Hope you understand.'

Paradoxically, it was after Raggadagga left that I had my strongest fusions with the environment. I feel now that the magic mushrooms merely opened up the channels – or the conceptual framework – within which the deep links I feel with the world around me could be established. The problem was that the drugs proved over time to provide rapidly diminishing returns. I took to making long lonely walks in my region. Where I live at Welham Green, footpaths and relatively underused metalled lanes radiate out in all directions: southwards towards the old Middlesex border; north across the Colne and onto the lower Chilterns; west towards London Colney and Watford; and east over the high and remote plateau beyond the BBC masts leading through to the barbarian colonies at Newgate Street and Cheshunt. I spent whole seasons chattering to Raggadagga, who walked alongside me in my imagination, despite being long gone from my life. I often felt sorry for myself but something rich and exhilarating rose out of the bare-faced obduracy of my predicament and the sometimes sullen and uncommunicative land: deep in the blackness of many a lonely and tearful afternoon, a richness surfaced, casting a rosy light over my inner landscape like the sun's morning bloom rising over the edge of the dark and barren world of night.

One sunlit and breezy afternoon I spent an hour watching a water skater through binoculars as it worked its way across the pond on Brookmans Park Golf Course. As I followed its epic voyage towards the pond's far side I entered a realm of flashing light. The surface movement of the water – the shifting facets of its wavelets – caught the sun's rays and concentrated them until they thickened, becoming a brilliant fiery ectoplasm. The so-called 'miracle of the ordinary' in vogue in therapy circles these days was ruptured by the molten energy of the ripples – there was no longer any 'ordinary' (had there ever been for me?). And the brave little *Gerris lacustris*, climbing purposively through to its insect destiny on a voyage up the vertical cliff of wavering sunlight – this was the unscheduled event, the world stretched to its fullness. For a brief time I became more than merely I. The dragonfly and the lacewing stared out through my eyes. I was the yellow iris growing by pollen-specked moats.

Everything nowadays speaks against the type of love I felt and still feel for Raggadagga; the world no longer tolerates such emotions but sees them as pathological. Possibly there had been a need to challenge assumptions about what love is and how to behave when 'in love', but I think that as a result one set of myths about the nature of love has simply replaced another: 'You can't love somebody until you love yourself'; 'You're in love with the idea of being in love'; 'You're trying to use someone to fix yourself' – all complete and utter rot, the slow creep of monadic instrumentality.

I wanted to live. I wanted to be a force of nature, the wind that buffets the oaks so they rear, their leaves swirling and hissing, rocking their wild untamed heads at the field's edge. I wanted to be the distant ocean's roar, not a silly little brook running through some municipal sports field. I know that Hertfordshire is a living and creating Mother. We must now dream alive the past and future, and we must return to the Mother if we want to truly live. I believe I have found a way.

I will place my neck on the railway track by Skimpans Farm. I will feel the irons sing and then boil, hear the whir of the approaching wheels, the rising drilling roar of the turbo-charged locomotive as it closes in and finally engulfs me.

8

NEWGATE STREET

BREATHE DEEPLY AND BRACE myself as I leave Gloria drinking her infusion of Melissa in the Dellsome Café. There is a desert ahead, a remote region calling and it's time to face it once again. My aim is to bridge the gap between Welham Green and the uplands south of Hertford to the east.

Downhill from Dellsome Lane lies a cluster of cream houses, a cottage estate built in the 1930s for Hertfordshire's increasing population of factory workers. I approach this now, crossing a small triangular green, along one side of which is a wooden bus shelter. A sudden wet squall claps my ears and I duck into the shelter to check my maps. The road is deserted and through double-glazed windows I see late Christmas trees and the glow of TVs. The sound of traffic drifting over from the A1(M) reminds me that not everybody is in hibernation. A group of fieldfares works its way across the quaggy plough land. The birds move forward a few yards as one and then turn together to follow a new direction. A pheasant runs across the road a hundred yards ahead; its rusted creaking cry is clearly audible above the sizzle of water soaking into the soil.

The land is beginning to hate me; I can sense it trying to stare me out. I expect sooner or later to be driven from farmyards with stones, dogs snapping at my heels. I know I will be blanked in convenience stores in villages seldom visited by anybody who could reasonably be described as sane. Not that I'll succumb without a fight. I plan to puncture tractor tyres, kick the foul-breathed farm dogs, and burn down barns in revenge. I will march across this land like a one-man infantry division, my course marked by columns of smoke rising above the treeline as the police choppers *chup-chup* overhead and snipers conceal themselves in the furze or behind decrepit caravans.

I take Bulls Lane to Skimpans Farm – Gloria's favourite spot – and then under the railway and through to the hamlet of Bell Bar. Here I cross the Great North Road and walk down a long dead-straight footpath seething with rabbits, passing the 1950s science-fiction atom mystery of the BBC transmission masts and their concrete and steel utility buildings. The path curves left across a tiny stream (probably the same one that blurts out into the open after passing beneath the Northampton Railway at Skimpans) and onto the edge of a broad level field. I'm on a bold and elevated watershed and, looking to the west, can see to the Pitstone Hills far off, near Tring. My map tells me that this is a local top end – 127 metres: I am really on the uplands now.

I sit and smoke but soon an imperative kicks in and I'm on my feet again, climbing a stile onto Kentish Lane and turning sharp right towards a concrete track that drills its way across a vast plateau of parcelled fields. I stand and stare at the lonely way stretching ahead as my breath mists my glasses. I shake my head and realise I can't go through with it. Something about the plateau fills me with foreboding. The imperative fades and I turn and head south for Potters Bar and a bus home, my heart sinking with the realisation of my own failure.

Perhaps it is a sense I have of the east as being somehow colder or more spiteful than the other cardinal points. East London, with its desperate estates and its vicious villainy; The Eastern Front during the Second World War, where armies were swallowed by snow, and whole peoples ravaged by famine; East Finchley, where D—— lived and I once got fined two quid for an overdue library book. The very word, when seen on the page somehow suggests bared teeth and impending skinhead violence: EAST.

I ponder this an hour later while sitting over a coffee in the Jenny Burger in Potters Bar. Whenever I think of Harefield and Moor Park, far off to the west, I see warm sunlit meadows or tasteful furnishings in timbered houses. The Eastern Marches however – particularly Hertford and the town of

Cuffley – invoke visions of nothing so much as white leather sofas and fat bottoms squashed into tracksuits. My prejudices and assumptions are disgusting I know, and I have no defence, but I find the East is lonely and feels far from home.

Now it is 8 July 2007 and I have returned for a second try. A steely mineral sun scorches the back of my neck as the land paranoia, the fear of this barren flinty earth grips hold. What if this route leads nowhere or I find myself sinking into the black muck of some cattle latrine all tangled in cleavers or nettles? Or suppose it finally dawns on me that I'm doomed as I lie broken in the barbed-wire ditch where I've fallen, my whole being a single dark wound throbbing unnoticed in the bone-dry landscape? I might collapse by a pylon, the cholesterol coagulating in my veins, until the farmer's dog runs up, sniffs around me and pisses on my leg. Then a crow waddles over to me and pecks out my eyes. Or some unnameable piece of farm-yard machinery grabs my T-shirt, pulls me into its clanking interior and slowly skins me alive. What would Scarp, my cruel indifferent mistress, have to say about that?

But Train Hard, Fight Easy, as Marshal Suvorov famously said; I have prepared for this day for months and, taking my compass in hand, I march off along the concrete track. After half a mile or so I come to a stone bridge propped on thick steel girders with a gulley running below. I lean over the para-pet and watch the water flowing northwards. Always interested in tracking rivers I reach into my rucksack and take out my OS map: the stream is the Essendon Brook and is joined later by a second stream rising further east known as the Wild Hill

Brook. Essendon; Wild Hill: the former I have visited a couple of times, the latter I have never heard of.

I remember some years back, hiking along the Hertford Road, following the north side of the grounds of Hatfield House as part of a two-day walk across Hertfordshire from Dunstable Downs. Bellowing came from the deer park on the other side of the wall of the estate and thousands of purple-blotched hemlock grew alongside the road. It had been a long and lonely walk, undertaken on one of those hot, sticky late summer days when the ants mate in mid-air and thunderstorms threaten. I was technically mad at the time and the darkness solidifying in my mind found its exact analogue in those moist, poisonous stems – I too felt like a danger lurking overlooked in the ostensibly pretty landscape.

I settled down that night under the old cedar growing in the churchyard at Essendon. After laying out my jacket and sleeping bag, I twisted the top off my whisky bottle and knocked back a mouthful. I drank and smoked as the evening drew in, accompanied by the plaintive triplets sung by a thrush perched in the top of an ash tree close by.

An alcohol-induced inner hush descended, its arrival corresponding with the quietening of the day. As the darkness grew, bringing safety and a more serene solitude, my contemplation of the weekend's walking became increasingly nuanced. I rolled a joint, the hash blowing a hole through the alcoholic muzz and rewarding me with a new clarity, a sense of the places through which I'd travelled that day. I thought about the long walk from the Five Knolls at Dunstable down through an undulating and steadily diminishing set of hills broken here and there by barge-boarded cottages and disused chalk quarries. I'd passed a domed concrete reservoir looking like some lesser *ouvrage* plucked from the Maginot Line and dropped into the heart of the Hertfordshire countryside. Then I came to Harpenden in the Valley of the Nightingales and followed the river Lea through Wheathampstead down to Hatfield.

But that was so long ago and now my world was larger, my knowledge greatly increased. Now I carried whole swathes of the region with me, wherever I walked. I was able to work through complex sequences of places in my mind as I lay in bed at night, linking up the different walks I'd made over the years. The towns visited on my journeys and the tracks and roads running between them stayed fixed, each in its mind-mapped place. There were low chalky corners of fields that seemed charged with an indefinable magnetism that drew me to them again and again. Other places seemingly possessed their own gloomy darkness or, for no apparent reason, felt fetid and miasmic but nevertheless attracted me precisely because of their power to induce such a sensation in me. I knew where badgers had died or caravans rotted away until mere stains of rust were all that remained.

But this glowering lonely land-bridge running between the Great North Road and the A10 further east remains a stranger however often I walk it. I try to fix in my mind the complex configuration of hills that make up this broad largely unpopulated eastern-central segment of Scarp but always come away from the effort no closer to the truth.

Towns like Potters Bar and North and South Mimms seem, in comparison to this high and mighty reaching towards clouds and unknowingness, to be mere extensions of the Barnet Universe, the Finchley Universe. I see the dwellers of these towns, hair streaming behind them as they zip past with car-roofs down, sunglasses worn like Alice bands. There is a claustrophobic certainty as to the value of things that manifests in the traffic-whipped lanes. And London always hovers in the background, its force-field rising like a tide over Scarp's spine before depositing its moraine of garden sheds, gaily striped recliners and denuded front gardens on the living, sloping surface of the land. The quiet streets that once so mystified me look all the same from up here – and this wide space before me as I trudge down the track speaks to me of something else.

A fieldpath runs off to the right and drops down towards Northaw, where the twelfth-century hermit Sigar told the birds to stop singing, the better to aid his meditations. When his funeral casket was brought to St Albans Abbey for burial the birds of the county flew in from all directions and formed a dark cloud overhead. During the Second World War there was a POW camp for Italian prisoners up here. Away to the left I can see the glint of motorway traffic in some far off place I have never been.

The concrete path passes alongside Barbers Lodge Farm. Here I sit on the iron steps of a concrete outhouse and admire the farm's old wooden barn, its timbers warped and smoothed by time. Cats wander about – I watch a particularly stringy ginger tom lurching across the farmyard from behind some rusted machinery.

Then I notice the half-built, flare-prowed yacht, mounted on wooden blocks in an open-ended shed so large it dwarfs the farmhouse alongside it. The boat perched on dry ground miles from any water; the sound of the boat-builders' hammering echoing across the fields: both heighten my sensation that this landscape is an overlooked or forgotten place within which the unusual and unexpected can still occur.

Further on, the track ascends to run along an elongated and level crest line. The tower blocks at Edmonton Green, in the Lea Valley, come into view. Further south I can see the soft curves of the Kentish Hills, a delicate dove blue from this distance. The effect is dramatic and humbling. Dramatic because it illustrates how elevated the plateau is, the view bringing in elements of four counties (Hertfordshire, Middlesex, Essex and Kent); humbling, because the eastern suburbs of London seem like delicate gossamer when viewed from this distance.

This is a thrown thing, this land. An unrecorded history hovers over the oily fat rape, the full-summer mallows with their seedpods like Dutch cheeses, the factories and hospitals in the river valley. Off to the left a track heads past a brick farmhouse with an extension that has seen better days. Just beyond is Tylers Causeway and roads leading down-slope to hornbeam groves and the hamlets of Wild Hill and West End.

I only discovered these places later, in February 2011, on a walk spent taking photographs of evening meadows and a solitary bare tree that rose to eternity on my computer desktop. It is a remote band of country, this northern edge of the plateau. My walk that day took me over the river valley and up Gypsy Lane (where Barbara Cartland established Barbaraville, a Romany gypsy camping site, in 1964) and through to new estates where I had to double back on myself because their interior roads all ended in cul-de-sacs. Then there were the dusky streets of Welwyn Garden City, through which rushed needle-straight chains of light – trains bound for Cambridge, Lincoln and the far north.

Eventually the concrete track becomes good solid roadway and houses begin to appear on either side. It is the edge of Newgate Street, a quiet easterly hamlet which sports a large Greek Orthodox community. It would be possible to reach Cuffley from here in an hour or so by turning off down Carbone Hill and then following the Cuffley Brook through Great Wood. I don't fancy it however. Carbone Hill is dangerous – images of cars smashing bone – and Cuffley an unfriendly sort of place. Besides, I want to stay up here in the heights, following Scarp as far to the north-east as I can manage today.

I take a track to the left past a pond and across my millionth field into the yard of a 1920s stud farm, built in the German colonial style. The light is softening and an unexpectedly chill wind rises, threatening rain. An electric gate – 'press button to open' – releases me onto the road to Epping Green. I pass through the village and half a mile further on the old brick houses of Little Berkhamsted appear. On the right is the local church. It is here that the Tory MP Reginald Maudling lies buried together with his wife.

As I stare down at the gravestones I hear a cough followed by spluttering and a wet stringy gob of mucus splatters on the ground at my feet. I turn my head in alarm and see a rough-faced relic from a bygone era sitting on one of the memorial benches busily trying to roll a cigarette with his shaking fingers. His clothes are dust-impregnated greys and browns, his hair a claggy bird's nest matted with filth.

'You got a light, sonny?' he asks, tilting his head back and pointing to me with his chin. I oblige, leaning over him but holding *my* head back, the better to avoid the smell.

'I didn't see you there. You frightened me,' I say awkwardly, sensing that he has spotted my reticence.

'Ay, I'll do that you'll find,' he replies, giving me a hard, cold look.

And then he starts.

*

You who see me walk the Watford by-pass in my filthy flasher mac. You who laugh at my foul-mouthed toothless muttering as you splash by me on Alum Lane, my ear stung by the half-empty Coke can you threw from your car window. You who refused me when I asked for water that hot day on the gravelly private road at Moor Park, taking me for a mere layabout, a schnorrer cadging for cigarettes or the price of a pint. You who see me as a mud-creature churned up out of the stodgy cold clay on some building site in Casio or Hertsmere.

You who laugh, you who fear, you who hate.

I was born John Osborne in 1700 at Gubblecote, near Tring in the county of Hertfordshire of yeoman stock and was fortunate to be educated in the rudiments of reading and writing, this provided by Mother Goodie at her Dame School. When I was ten my schooling ended and, shying from the hard labours undertaken by my father, I took to wandering the lanes near my home, watching the yearly cycle of flowers in their change from yellow and white through purple to shrivelled brown. I poked ants' nests with sticks, watched closely the bibble-bugs rolling into balls, crouched frightened and transfixed by the hot papery fury of the hornets' nest under the stone pillars supporting the barn.

My friends the Midsummer Men would meet me then, at the lower end of the Slipe, where the dock-leaves and tall dusty nettles sheltered crickets from the sun's rays and the dead pigeon pulsed with maggots. These Tom-peep Gentlemen would take me down through the white-flowered devil's guts into the net of ditches and the acorn's kernel. In winter, too, my friends would whisper to me, enjoining me to leave my body and follow them under molehills or into old pipes packed with snails deep in winter sleep. They were my familiars, these Odd People, and I knew them better than my old father bent with thrashing in the fields, or my mother sitting blind at her spinning wheel in the cottage. Even good old Atticus, who always jumped up and wheezed and slobbered on seeing me at the day's end, his tail beating the wall, was as a stranger in comparison.

Then suddenly, one hot day, my friends were gone. That morning, I turned the corner of the lane anticipating the usual greeting from myriad voices but instead heard nothing more than the furious trillo of a black bee trapped under a leaf, the rising hysteria of the wood pigeon's call. Unsettled, I sat and waited for my companions by the road to Aylesbury, my back resting against the chalk milestone. Later, I went looking for them in the splintering willows down by the brook, rushing from place to place until my face was whipped raw by the lash of blackberry bushes. No one came, no one called me and I ran home crying and fell weeping into the arms of my poor blind mother, who, taking me into the kitchen, fed me honey cakes and mollified me with the spinning top my uncle bought for me in Dunstable. The following day I joined my father in the fields and over the next few months gained in yeoman skills and those of good husbandry. As time passed my friends seemed to grow vague in my memory and finally I forgot them.

After a period spent cavorting and gaining the pleasures of the flesh in my early adulthood, I took me a wife, Ruth Goodwife, living with her happily in a cottage on the glebe. Later my father and mother died and were laid to rest in the churchyard at Tring. Then one day I found Atticus lying dead in the long sedge down where the elders grow by the pond. It was while I knelt crying and holding his dear little paw in my hand that my friends spoke again, their voices mingling with the buzzing of the green-bottles settling on Atticus's snout and the *zic-zic* of a grasshopper's love call somewhere in the fretting chervils.

'We are waiting for you,' they said. And, 'Come meet us at the birch at the lower end of the Slipe field each dawn.' That

day I felt as if I lived again, though I had never even realised I had been dead. The next morning I rushed across the
fields to the leafless old birch. The tree's slender white trunk
and branches were visible from afar and called to the spirit in
me with a stronger voice than the crucifixes I saw in the cold
miserable churches of Dunstable or Gaddesden. And there they
waited, the Thimble Men, the Pin Men, the Tumble Tots with
their whispers and charms.

That day I began my instruction, a journey that took me on
visits to deep libraries, archives stored in fallen leaves, snapped
mossy twigs, insect addled middens. I learned many new things
over the following months and years but as a result I grew
strange and remote from the world of men with its tobacco
pipes and newspapers, its fine carriages, laces and prize pigs.
I learned to keep company for the most part with spiders and
millipedes, the pale blue scorpion grass and that fine upright
fellow Johnny-Go-to-Bed-at-Noon, liking nothing better than
to join him in sleep under a tree when the sun grew too hot, my
thoughts blowing away across the county into the blue distances
of the southern hills like dried leaves snatched by the wind.

I taught what I knew to Ruth and patiently worked the fields
for Mr Jasper year by year while she sowed and cooked. We
kept cats and also a pet beetle in a japanned box. *These were
our friends you understand*. We grew herbs in our little plot
or gathered them in moonlight from the surrounding countryside. Ruth attended to the curing of both illiterate villager
and ailing animal, grinding roots and lard into poultices with a
pestle and mortar or standing over simmering decoctions. And

so the years passed and we grew older. *But still we carried on with our works.*

The world of men continued in its turmoil however, and troubles far from Gubblecote bore down on us when I was about forty-five years old. A pretender to the throne whipped up his people to a fury far to the north and began to head south, intent on seizing London Town. The King's army rose to meet him in the field. Columns of red coats marched through the village and settled, singing and drinking each night around campfires until the whole vale resounded with the yahoo of their debauchery. Then they were gone. For days afterwards riders rode south carrying urgent messages to the King and his parliament. The cost of the war in the north was high, taxes were demanded to pay for powder and steel and things were tight. Often Ruth and I went hungry.

One June day Ruth asked John Butterfield, a local farmer, for some buttermilk fresh from the cow as charity and on being refused by that arrogant and self-righteous man, foolishly cursed both Butterfield and his animals, saying that the Pretender (whom many saw as the Devil) would pay him out. Her fury, focused through the lens of her will by the force of her utterance, became a piercing white beam capable of altering the very substance of the world, as I had been taught and had passed on to her. Heat grew and vapours rose. Over the next week Butterfield started to suffer fits and contagion took the cows. I was furious with Ruth and challenged her judgement in this affair, begging her to reverse her work but this – as I knew – she could not do. I worried most that our happy lives would be forfeit as a result, and in this I was to be proved correct.

Forced to retire from farming because of his affliction, Butterfield took up as an innkeeper and turned to drink. There were mutterings and complaints in Gubblecote and Tring over his fate and Ruth and I were shunned by many who formerly greeted us as friends. The services we provided were no longer required and because of this food became ever shorter. I grew scared when I heard tell of pamphlets concerning Ruth and myself being handed around on market days and letters branding us as evil being handed to Dell, the Hempstead crier. I knew it was on top and that this affair with Butterfield would never be forgotten until we'd paid.

One April day there came a vast crowd armed with staves led by the drunken chimneysweep Thomas Colley. They gathered about the cottage, shouting and cursing, calling for Ruth and me to come out. Seeing no other way, we did so, hoping to reason with the crowd but, spurred on by the rattish Colley, they would have none of it. Then there were blows and spitting, men pissing on our poor furniture, hen coops overturned, our beloved cats caught and strangled before us. Ruth and I were punched and beaten until we could barely stand and were then carried by the baying horde down to a pond at a place called Marlston Green. Ruth was thrown into the water while the crowd booed and cheered and pelted her with stones. I was punched to the ground by the farrier Richard Redbeard of Leyton Buzzard and forced to watch. I will never forget what happened next. Ruth sank upon hitting the water and then came to the surface, spluttering and flailing as she struggled to stay afloat. Her body was weighed down by her dress, her face twisted as she gasped for air. 'She floats!' the crowd screamed and the foul Colley, who had been busy collecting coins for the entertainment provided, leaned out over the edge of the pond and prodded her with his stave, repeatedly forcing her under and then letting her rise again. Blood seeped from the cuts on Ruth's brow and her quick breath, gained upon each surfacing, began to falter and then stopped. Finally she rolled over and lolled face-down in the Jenny Green-Teeth as her struggle ceased. Then it was my turn.

I was in such despair at what I'd just witnessed that I was ready to die and join Ruth then and there, but it was not to be. As the cold water closed over my head and darkness swam behind my eyes a troop of the King's dragoons arrived and broke up the crowd with the flats of their swords, arresting the ringleaders. I was pulled from the pond and taken to kindly Mr Lucas's house where I was revived with warm blankets and brandy.

I survived to see Colley hanged for murder at Hertford, watching the frantic circles drawn by his tethered legs as he choked on the rope. His body was brought to Gubblecote and chained to a gibbet to warn off further cases of mobbery. Broken in spirit and no longer able to face what remained of the happy home I had kept with Ruth, I wandered off to find work where I could, leaving Gubblecote for ever. The good Clutterbucks of Hitchin employed me awhile as a storekeeper but let me go after receiving threats from the people of that fine town. I turned to the parish for alms and was handled roughly with insults and beatings for my bread and broth, repaying five times over in labour in the workhouse for the mere scavengings I received.

People say I died in the workhouse some years later but this is not true. During the time spent in that dung heap I practised arts and rituals both complex and efficacious, as had been taught to me by my companions, the Bead-headed Ones. When ready I dissolved my form and simply merged into the summer backdrop of horehound and hardheads, the ill-disciplined tracery of bryony and ivy and bindweed. Years went by and I was nothing more than a murmur in the tops of those mad horses, the wind-whipped elms. I was a cold feeling in a gloomy lane, something that slid into darkened bedrooms and stood rasping and clicking over paralysed sleepers. My friends the good fellows kept me company during the time spent on the world's underside, preparing me for works darker than those to which I had once been accustomed.

I resurfaced one day, slipping out of a chunk of puddingstone near the village of Bayford in south Hertfordshire. I had learned by now to preserve my age – fifty-two – and took to wandering the uplands thereabouts before settling down as a farmhand at Elstree. For twenty years I worked the fields until my employer, Thomas Marsh, went mad, drooling on his deathbed and raving at my timeless features. 'You are the very Devil, Sir,' he shouted, staring at me in terror through bulging eyes. The doctor in attendance fixed me with a piercing look and in order to avoid any unnecessary trouble I slipped away that night with nothing more than bread and cheese to sustain me.

Worrying about a possible hue and cry I avoided St Albans and Hertford – those vulgar and spiteful hanging towns – and with increasing frequency took to burying myself alive and passing into long trances, thereby fast-forwarding the years a dozen at a time, as I had been shown. In this way I attempted to run further from the memory of poor cold Ruth. I woke to steam trains, to mechanical farming methods, to motorcars. Metalled roads unravelled across the country like ribbons, and pylons slung their fizzing charges through the trees. I haunted the hills south of Hertford, making my living by fixing camshafts and engine cylinders, stereophonic radiograms and television sets and – when times were difficult – shrinking myself at nights to fit in the warm security of feather and moss-packed boles in the oak trees that marked the corners of fields.

But I never escaped Ruth's death.

Another war – this larger than any previously seen – erupted in Europe and the village men, the shoemakers, clerks, labourers and brewers, marched off down the dusty lanes to disappear for ever. I saw Zeppelins bomb the towns on the scarp, flares and tracer light the pitch-black night and joined my friends again to avoid being pressed into the King's service.

You are not to think I feared death, you who sneer at my rummaging in bins in Watford or Borehamwood, my sweat-faced shouts at Hare Krishna soup kitchens, my hacking and hawking in A&E departments. I care nothing for these struggles you set such great store by, be they in the Scottish highlands, some treeless island chain in the south Atlantic or the mountains of Afghanistan. With Ruth's death my lack of interest in the world of human affairs hardened into hatred. I drew a thin black line across the world and waited, tensed, knowing that one day one of you would pry just a little too closely into my workings, my procedures.

This was a line crossed by that philanderer John Child in the winter of 1941 when I blew his brains and dentures all over his little park-keeper's shack at Moat Mount with a Webley .455 after he caught me emerging like a vapour from a concrete post by the Leg-o-Mutton lake where I had spent the previous ten years communing with that sprite Isabella Mouldytits. This was my first killing. When I watched the ineptitude of the police in their efforts to apprehend the murderer I just laughed, clutching my ribs and chuckling in the bed-sitting room I took in Carpenders Park. The poor sods thought Child had been murdered by a cuckold.

I didn't stick around too long that time. The ranting of madmen in Europe, the twin-engined bombers flying in mass formation, the uniforms and insignia, torch-lit processions and window-smashing: these spoke to me of looming disasters, still further insanities.

The next to cross the line was the plumber Albert Welch in 1947, after he stumbled across me as I rose from the dried-out stems of a burdock one winter's night on Brookmans Park Golf Course. I bound and carved him, relieving him of his tongue, which I ate before dumping his bits and pieces in the pond by Flinter's Wood, my second killing. I also crossed a

line that night, moving into a new inner landscape as I realised I had developed a taste. It felt fine, this inflicting of pain
and torture, this settling of accounts. I loped past the metal
flag marking the golf course's 17th tee and headed east, crossing the Great North Road, and climbed onto the long line of
remote ridges which rose darkly ahead. I sat smoking that
night in belts of dead ferns, mesmerised by the scintillations
of the distant A roads and by-passes. Needless to say the
London police travelled north by train, hanging around on
the golf course in their Daks and trilbies but found nothing
of use.

I rejoined the world of men, finding work where I could
and secure in the knowledge that I could leave again, anytime
I liked. One wet and miserable evening at the fag-end of 1957
I visited Marshalls Heath Lane, near Wheathampstead and
left my body in order to undertake some important task under
instruction from my secret friends. I shrank down and merged
into a hedgerow, fusing with plant memories, bird thoughts
and insect politics. I whiled the time in a kind of colourful
electrically lit cellular flow that linked me up with the whole
region, my compound eyes staring from ditches, a watcher
through weeds. I became a mere coin for my Queen's expendi-
ture, a goat-man unnoticed. I was a spotted ladybird trapped in
a car, dead newspapers in attics, a broken swing hanging from
an apple tree in the garden of a derelict house and the curve
in a country lane crossed by millions of young frogs bound
for entropic ponds. Finally, emerging as a purring winter moth,
my work complete, I slipped back into my usual form only

to find a podgy young woman standing in front of me. The look on her face told me that she'd seen everything and I leapt, clutching her fluttering throat with my strong timeless hands. I dumped her body into the back of my van and drove off before she was missed.

I hid her in a freezer at the British Oxygen Company in Edmonton where I had a job as warehouseman. The girl's disappearance made the news and one night at the cinema I was shocked to see her face flash up on the screen, the image accompanied by a crackling request, asking members of the public to report any sighting of her to the police. Hertfordshire was torn apart in the search for the missing girl and I knew it would come on top unless I got rid of her soon. It was a mild winter, with hardly any snow, otherwise I would've dumped Anne's body out in the fields near her home in the hope the police would think she'd died of exposure. Instead I drove north to Hitchin and laid her out on the grass in some woods where she was discovered two days later.

After that I gave up my job and flat and melded with a manhole cover in an alleyway in Queens Avenue, Finchley. I stayed fixed through the 1960s, an inscribed steel pentagram bedded amidst the cinders and snails, the cats and weeds. One day my flat metallic face stared out at a small bespectacled boy who walked past. I became a hissing poisonous thought and shadowed him between blank brick walls and alongside creosoted fences. He made his way down to an electricity substation at the alley's end, where he stood looking through the fence at fish moving silently in a pond. I followed him to his house nearby and gazed in at him as he sat watching television with his family that night. My hands itched to choke him out of spite but I never had the chance.

I returned to my human body in 1970 and found a disillusioned country, the national football team huffing and sulky, brat-faced pop stars grown ill and angry and a grinning teddy bear of a Prime Minister helpless to stem the decline in moral standards. Thirteen-year-old Philippa Gordon joined my select gang of initiates in November 1975 when she unfortunately accepted a lift from me along the Watford Way and ended up, her neck snapped like a linnet's, buried near the rabbit holes along Sandy Lane by the M1, my fourth killing. And there she lays still, the blank page of her destiny overwritten by millions of thoughtless car journeys, by shopping trips, computer games, Capitol Gold, by electronic *yack-yack-yack*.

About that time I gave up on caring how you see me, you who stand before me in your ridiculous shorts, your car bonnet beer-spattered by the can I threw after you nearly knocked me down at the Busy Bee Roundabout. I forsake the workings of the human world; thrive on handouts and estovers drawn from bins at the backs of shops. I spit on you, sir, though you grab my filthy, infested hair and pummel me, your slag-faced girlfriend egging you on.

In this I'm helped by the whisky and the fags.

I plug the sopping fields and the sodden stiles, clay mounting on my rotten boots as I trace the crestline that divides the Brent-bound and Colne-bound riverlets. I pass the usual walkers, those myopic nerdies with their hard-boiled eggs wrapped in handkerchiefs, their 'pinch of salt' and banana or organic oatcake packed away in their hideous cheap rucksacks. I hate them and could murder them, their trillibubs hanging red and stinking from sliced bellies, their cracked lips curling back over yellow teeth, their blood-specked glasses left poking out of a cowpat for a laugh.

I walk within yards of Erica Treadwell, aged seventeen, tarpaulin-wrapped and buried deep in December 1984, after I stripped and slashed her in sight of dog-walkers and parked cars near Newgate Street. It was there, on the sorry gravels, the rain-flogged plateau dividing the Great North Road from the valley of the river Lea as it curves southwards into Ware, that I realised first the full measure of my affliction. One day I will come down off the hills early, only stopping to urinate against an oak tree standing in the corner of a field. I will be aiming, as is my habit, to walk the dank tiled subway below the A road and head to the nearest town for fags and a straightener before spending an hour or two by the station, my hands out in supplication. On this day, though it will be different. Alarmed, my blood chilling even as I zip up, I see them emerge from behind the furze, these healthy ones with their ironed jeans, their smart leather jackets and crackling radios. They come at me from all directions, six or seven of them, their analytic eyes fixed on me, knowledge of at least one aspect of my nature showing in their determination to hold me in their steely grip. Then I will spot the police cars parked discreetly in the lane nearby. And I will be a rat scurrying into a fetid runnel. I will be unrecorded ant dynasties and the life cycle of transparent freshwater shrimps. I will travel below time and resurface when ready, my disappearance attributed to simple human stealth, my escape an embarrassment to the Hertfordshire Constabulary.

9

SOUTHGATE

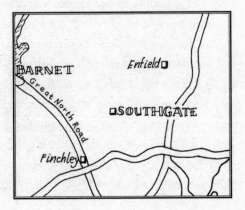

A S THE AFTERNOON TRAFFIC piled up at the junction of the North Circular and the Great North Road, I crawled through the thicket of elders to the pavement's edge and poked my head out in the hope of finding someone – a friend returning home from school perhaps – to break the day's tedium. It was sometime early in 1971 and I'd been hiding from the greenies in my little patch of wasteland behind the houses on Glebe Road, Finchley.

Behind me the black smoke from the fire I'd built earlier that afternoon coiled through the dried-out brakes of burdock, the hooked stems of teasel. It was damp and freezing and I was hungry. I was also desperately tired, my attempt to sleep away the school hours in the little shack I'd made out of old doors and sheets of iron having been defeated by the cold.

I lived out my truant days in a tiny space wedged between traffic flows and manoeuvred through pauses in the torrent of steel on my brief excursions out of the wasteland into the world. The continuous sound of traffic formed the backdrop to my playing and reading, the drone overriding my labouring breath as I attempted to inflate the space-hopper I'd dragged out of the thistles. This day it was particularly relentless due to major roadworks a mile to the east at Colney Hatch Lane, where the old roundabout – in the centre of which there grew an ash tree planted to celebrate the opening of the North Circular in 1936 – was being gouged out of existence by power shovels and the foundation of a new flyover pile-driven into the underlying London clay.

There was no one I knew in sight, only a pair of women chatting as they headed in the direction of the fire station, and suddenly, sickening of my exile in the waste ground, I hauled myself up onto the pavement and headed off to pinch a Mars bar from the confectioner's nearby. As I pulled my coat tighter about me to keep out the freezing wind the traffic halted and a panda pulled up alongside me. I glanced round and saw the driver, a sour-faced policewoman, staring at me in distaste. I pushed down a mounting panic and walked on, trying to appear as normal as possible. I expected any second to hear the sound of feet closing behind me, an 'Excuse me, love, shouldn't you be in school?' as the copper grasped my arm. Finally, looking round, I saw the policewoman still firmly seated at her steering wheel. She was busy speaking through the car window to a woman in a Messerschmitt cabin-scooter parked alongside and seemed to have no interest in me. I hurried on towards the crossroads.

I turned the corner and looked back to check whether the policewoman had followed me onto the Great North Road. The cars were moving again and I saw her panda disappearing down the North Circular towards Friern Barnet: I could relax.

As I stood there, watching the traffic curl away, my eyes fixed on the broached spire of a pale stone church poking above the raised skyline of houses visible on the far side of the tangled wooded depths of old Finchley Common. It was not the first time I'd seen it – it had been an element in the landscape from my earliest childhood, but was so familiar that it had become a mere component part of the backdrop to my life, a distant presence staring down on all this traffic hum, acid slush and grey silt of exhaust fumes.

Suddenly the distant spire was lit up by a shaft of sunlight that pierced the otherwise unbroken ceiling of cloud. And this remote and austere structure was transformed by the golden light into a glowing arbor, a timeless pivot around which revolved in all its momentariness the maelstrom of traffic, the crop-haired and tie-dyed violence of my school life, and the louche antics of the adult world that controlled me.

I had perhaps a vague sense that I was looking towards the heights of Southgate, one of those places *unknown* that hovered mysteriously beyond my familiar streets and parks, exposure to which threatened to tip the little world I had mapped out over the years into a larger, more turbulent continuum. True, there were kids in my class at school who came from Southgate, but my own experience of the place was limited to a single visit to its swimming pool with my elder brother and sister in the summer of 1968. It was a day I preferred to forget – on the way home we'd popped in at a sweetshop in North Finchley and, much to my siblings' disgust, I'd been caught nicking a packet of chewing gum. It wasn't the act of theft that annoyed them but my complete amateurishness in the affair and the resulting embarrassment.

Though the spire remained unchanged and firmly rooted in its given spot I found that for some reason I was drawn to it and unexpectedly taken back to an earlier time, to events I had previously forgotten. It must have been during the early 1960s, when young men still dressed in dark suits and ties, the elderly mainly in black. There were fewer cars in those days and trolley buses still sparked up and down the main streets of Finchley. I was being wheeled in a pushchair by my mother from the family home in Queens Avenue, downhill to the Great North Road. Here we boarded a bus – 'hold very tight, please' *ding-ding* – and off we went, the bus passing through places forgotten for purposes I wouldn't have understood at that age. I had a vague memory of broad sports fields and rows of houses slipping past but not much more. And then somehow, after an indeterminate time, we were back where we'd boarded, having completed what seemed like a great circle. Pivotal to the whole memory, as I recalled it both in 1971 and as I write this now, was the same church spire, perched like some inscrutable owl at the dead centre of, and visible from nearly all points on the journey we'd made.

As I stood there, recalling the earlier event, I felt – probably for the first time – an overwhelming sense of my mother's absence. Comparing the grizzled existence I lived now with childhood memories of my family life, I could only wonder at how badly things had gone downhill since. Whereas once we had all sat together every evening around the campfire of the TV set, now there was nothing other than continual cold and hunger. My father, driven near insane by poverty, ill health and the demands of his children, reached all to readily for the belt or an old poker left over from the days when we could afford coal.

And the world too seemed to have passed through a downward curve into slovenly indulgence and bare-faced avarice. Yet in spite of everything that had happened, the church had remained unmoved; it was a silent sentinel that watched over all this decay, all this loss of restraint. Years later I came to realise that the heights on which the church stood were the southern face of a promontory of Scarp that has its roots at Ferny Hill some miles to the north.

After my mum left home in 1966, I turned to my army of Airfix model soldiers for solace. I would refight the battles of Austerlitz or Borodino on my bedroom carpet, casualties inflicted by throwing matchsticks at the columns of Russian and French infantry, the loose packs of light cavalry working round the flanks of the opposing armies. War was all I knew of time and history and I had enough awareness of the world by then to know we lived beneath the shadow of a future, final conflict. As for my family history – it was something I had no sense of. My grandparents on both sides were dead I'd been told and that was that.

Later though – in the 1980s – I began to wonder about these things. Obviously, given my name, my father came from Greece and this fact rendered any desire I may have had to research my grandparents on his side extremely difficult. Years later I found a photograph of him on page 184 of *The War in Pictures, Volume 2* published by Odhams Press during the war years. He was one of a group of soldiers of the Epirus Army servicing a Hotchkiss mountain gun in Albania – I would've recognised his miserable expression anywhere.

My mother, on the other hand, was English – a pure Londoner – and had emerged out of a community still living somewhere in the streets about me but rendered anonymous by time and indifference. I drew a blank whenever I thought of my mum's own parents. I seemed to recall her rather dolefully telling me her parents died during the war, possibly as a result of enemy action.

In 1992, aged thirty-three, I bought a copy of my birth certificate from Somerset House for the purposes of obtaining a passport. The document revealed that my mum had been married before she met my dad, to a Polish man named Edward Kwiczala. This was a surprise – something I had known nothing about – but otherwise told me little. I remained stranded, washed up in a life that bore no tangible connection to the community around me.

In the mid-2000s I finally decided to get to the bottom of the issue of my mother and her parents and spent several days trawling through the endless shelves of birth and death books at the Family Record Office, at that time located in Farringdon. Birth dates were relatively easy to ascertain and provided no real surprises though the names and places I eventually retrieved were evocative: my mother, Josephine Hilda Ainge, born 1931 to Frances Ellen and James Honiwell Ainge in the Friern Barnet Urban District; my grandmother born 1903 in the Freehold Estate, also in Friern Barnet, her parents being John Cobley and Ellen Rowbotham.

The Freehold was a sump-pit of a place. Originally a few rows of dreary brick houses located in a belt of low land adjacent to a sewage farm, most of the old estate was demolished in the 1970s to be replaced by blocks of low-rise flats. I visited the Freehold several times in the months following the discovery of its connection to my past. A particular view across a park towards the bridge carrying the King's Cross Railway over the North Circular Road evoked vague memories of a family visit to the area one Saturday in the early 1960s. A sense of someone we'd sat down and had Sunday lunch with that day writhed behind the thick glass of the years but who it was remained – and still remains – infuriatingly evasive.

The dates of my grandparents' deaths continued to elude me. The death books from the 1940s bore no reference to them. Neither did those from the 1930s or '50s. Puzzled, and for the sake of completion, I decided to proceed as far forward in time as possible, despite my having no confidence that this would lead me anywhere. Imagine my shock, then, when I discovered that my grandfather, homeless and alcoholic, had been found dead on the pavement of Leigh Street, St Pancras in the winter of 1984. This was troubling, as I'd staggered that way almost daily in the early 1980s, on my way to buy opiated cough mixture from a chemist in Judd Street. It was possible that I'd unknowingly passed within yards of my grandfather. I wondered if I'd answered his drunken curses with my own stream of intoxicated oaths.

Worse, my grandmother died in a care home in Edmonton in 1994, within a hundred yards of the railway that carried me every weekday to my studies at the Middlesex University campus in Enfield. The death certificate included a record of her next of kin, the person whose name was entered being listed as her daughter, my mother's elder sister. When I read this I felt a great door opening on a lost past. My aunt's address was given as Lonsdale Avenue in Southgate and, after looking this street up in my 1962 *Bartholomew's Reference Atlas of Greater London*, I decided to walk there from High Barnet – a place I knew all too well – thus mirroring the shift from familiarity to the unknown in a walk.

I set off from my home in Childs Hill on a freezing cold November day, walking northwards through Golders Green, Finchley and Whetstone and on to Barnet. I climbed the giant ramp built to carry the Great North Road to that town, its grey castellated church tower visible ahead. High (or 'Chipping')

Barnet doesn't interest me overly, though some of the old brick factories and warehouses in its back streets speak of a Hertfordshire town that once possessed a coherent identity of its own. Barnet's northern reaches fray out to common land intersected by ditches in which, in May, Marsh marigolds grow in abundance. Further north I turned to the right and walked through the village of Monken Hadley, with its grand Georgian houses and its church famously topped by a copper beacon designed to guide travellers across what was once relatively remote country. Monken Hadley is a straggling and opaque village; its walled villas revealing nothing of the lives lived within.

I resisted the urge to approach Southgate through the dense oak and hornbeam-shrouded Hadley Wood. I'd walked about the place a few times before in the company of friends and their dogs and wanted on this occasion to experience a sense of defamiliarisation that correlated with my approaching meeting with my aunt. With this in mind, I crossed the gravelly upper level of Monken Hadley Common onto Camlet Way, a long straight road that connects Barnet with Enfield to the east. I have heard claims that Camlet Way takes its name from Camulodunum, the Roman name for Colchester, and is an old Roman route linking Sulloniacae in Stanmore with that town. I somehow doubt that this is correct but it is an intriguing idea. I hit the new suburb of Hadley where in two or three years' time I would be stopped and questioned by the police as a suspected terrorist. The large Victorian houses on either side of Hadley blurred into one another and I recall no real details of what I saw.

I turned southwards along Cockfosters Road, mesmerised like a rabbit by the chains of headlights approaching me. I wanted to hug closely to the sodium-lit and busy streets, the respectable cul-de-sacs and large old houses divided into flats. I think the idea was to immerse myself in the medium I imagined my aunt habitually moved in, as if in preparation for the meeting we had arranged by phone the previous day. It was only mid-afternoon but the light was bad and a cold damp wind blew in from the east, chilling me. This I liked: I demanded something more invigorating than a quiet suburban stroll in clement weather. My world was being torn open and I expected the elements to accord.

At one point I noted the land dropping away steeply from either side of the road and realised that the route I was taking led along what was in effect a narrow and extended causeway. Of Scarp as such I knew nothing at that time, though what was to occur that afternoon and evening was later to be seen as a transmission straight from its heart, a gift bestowed.

After passing Cockfosters Station I came to a long suburban shopping parade. The absence of supermarkets and charity shops was striking – was it a *real* high street, or somewhere that was maintained strictly for heritage purposes? Certainly, the shops seemed busy enough but what really staggered me was that this place had existed all my life, within a mere three or four miles of where I had spent my formative years, and yet was an utter stranger to me.

Cat Hill came and went and Cockfosters Road became Chase Side. Oaks – residues from when the road had been a mere country lane – still lined the route. Curve-windowed 1930s houses and blocks of luxury flats with sleek metal-railed balconies formed the backdrop to the incessant traffic. I passed a sports ground on the left, a tall brutalist clock tower peering out at me over the urinal hut, and belts of holly trees behind a stone wall on the right – the grounds of Oakwood Theological College. Then I cut left down Green Road, a terrifyingly silent street about which I now recall nothing else.

And so to Lonsdale Avenue and my aunt's large and scrupulously well-maintained house. I pressed the doorbell and watched through textured glass as someone approached from the other side. The door opened to reveal an elderly and bespectacled woman. I examined her appearance closely but found nothing to evoke any great emotion in me beyond the merely abstract understanding of our relationship. Fortunately I had not expected otherwise – any notion I may have had of my returning to a secure heartland of family life had been reasoned away by common sense. We sat down together in the large comfortable living room and began to talk.

A lot passed between us that afternoon. My aunt needed to hear that her sister died in December 1975. She told me that she'd known this somehow. I told her about myself and my somewhat chequered past. During the course of the afternoon my aunt mentioned that her husband had run a local sweet-shop on Alderman's Hill in the mid-1960s. I later realised that back in 1967, aged nine, during a day spent with my father at Broomfield Park, just to the south of Southgate, I'd visited a confectionery in a parade of shops close by and bought, for sixpence, a World Cup Willy football game, a leftover from the previous year's competition. It is possible that the man who had served me all those years ago was my aunt's husband.

She also told me about her childhood, how her father had been led off in a drunken stupor by the police in 1936 and never returned to the family. My grandmother worked at Standard Telephones & Cables on Bounds Green Road. In 1944 the factory was hit by a doodlebug, the explosion killing many of the workers. My mother and her sister spent that evening outside the smashed plant waiting to find out whether their mother had survived. Finally she emerged from behind the tapes placed to demark the incident site, white with dust from the pulverised walls and stone deaf for months afterwards.

As for my mother, she had left Edward Kwiczala – and their daughter – in 1952, after beginning an affair with my father. They'd met at Simms Motor Units in Finchley, where my mother worked as a nurse. My half-sister Tanya was raised by her father, my aunt and my grandmother, but was placed into foster care at my mother's instigation three years later. My aunt met my mother by chance one day in 1960 at Tally Ho Corner in Finchley. My mum was pushing a pushchair in which there sat a small blond-haired boy – almost certainly my elder brother George.

My aunt knew nothing of the details of my mother's eventual fate – how she'd suffered a double mastectomy, her breasts replaced by a pair of tin plates – I recalled catching a glimpse of one when her bikini-top accidentally slipped during an outing to Margate in 1974. It was a dented sad thing, a paltry substitute for what had been surgically removed.

The last time I'd seen her was after boarding a bus in Bromley in November 1975 after spending a weekend with her. I was clutching a potted plant she'd given me and I looked back at her from the platform of the Routemaster as it sped away. Her body was bloated by the lymph that had accumulated below her skin. She looked tired and defeated and I fought down a rising panic, a sense that we were truly saying goodbye. A week later I was in prison and within the month she was dead.

My aunt never forgave her sister for deserting Tanya. She returned to the subject repeatedly and I could understand why. Yet there was nothing to be done about her anger. Finally, things reached their conclusion and, armed with prints of my mother taken from her childhood, I put on my coat, turned up my collar and took my leave.

Once out on the street I headed north again, back up the Cockfosters Road, intending to take a train from Hadley into town to meet a friend. It was evening now and a tube train sparked as it entered Cockfosters Station. The evening traffic halted as the lights turned red, and dark faceless crowds emerged from the station before scattering to bus stops and shops. Further along the road stood the snagged stumps of oaks marking the edge of the green belt. I looked out on the blackened fields beyond and thought of the recently reported Beast of Enfield Chase, a large wildcat said to live thereabouts. The lights changed once more and traffic rushed past at high speed. To see these cars flash by, each a bubble of worry holding out the darkness of the night, is to see our world stretched over its abyss. The faltering day is a net, woven by our terms – a moment of mass hallucination, electrically lit, like the parade of shops across the way, against the blackness of some silent, patient noumenon.

*

The sweat wagon rattled through sequences of streets I would never know, my head hammering each time I rested it against the speckled plastic partition in front of me, the better to shut out the city's magnitude. Each turning in the road, each length of faceless housing, garishly lit filling station or greasy playing field, piled another layer on the bulwark now separating me from my old life. We approached Brentford and I was terrified by the colossal white tower blocks, the heaps of scrap cars, the flyover jammed with vehicles. Everywhere spoke of the world's misery, though years later (had I known it) south-west Middlesex was to become one of my select topographic hunting grounds. We crossed the heart of Hounslow Heath (I only knew this because I overheard a prisoner who came from the area taking an inventory of crimes committed in each locale) and East Bedfont (the name spotted on a shopfront). Looking out across the landscape I was struck by how flat it was. Lines of winter cabbages stood in fields and receded further than I could ever go now. I longed to follow these ranks of vegetables to little spinneys seen a half mile off, to warm-lit farmhouses or imagined barns. But the journey wound on its relentless course and as we approached our destination restlessness became evident in my fellow travellers. Talk became louder and I heard someone pondering which wing he would be placed in 'this time'.

Somewhere up ahead lurked darkness, a compression of hard faces, harsh voices, tattooed knuckles. I imagined the contempt at my valueless crime, the punch delivered in the shower room, the crunch of prison-issue work boot on dislodged spectacles, my watch pulled from bony wrist, shampoo filched, tobacco twisted from weak hands.

After passing over a level crossing, we entered a maze of small houses and bungalows. I saw a man open his garden gate and enter accompanied by a black Labrador. He didn't even notice us. We turned a final corner and, breaking free of the buildings, came to a vast expanse of wire fencing mounted on concrete posts and topped with coils of razor wire. The sweat wagon pulled up at a gate made of the same material. A screw wearing a heavy black raincoat came out of a little wooden hut and spoke to the driver briefly and then the gate slid open. We drove through and came to a halt in front of a five-storey zig-zagging edifice of filthy brown brick that stretched away in either direction. Each of its windows was barred, their sills smothered with belts of glinting wire. It was easily the largest building I had ever seen.

A group of three large Lebanese cedars stood on the other side of the car park. They seemed incongruous in such a situation. A line of poplars edged the remand centre's grounds to the left and on the far side of the trees I could see car lights streaking rapidly along a modern arterial road. Further off – a mile or so distant – a lit office block rose above the landscape.

After a few minutes a particularly severe-looking screw wearing a white shirt rather than the usual blue emerged from the entrance of the building and mounted the bus.

'Is there anyone on board up for murder or rape?' he yelled.

With this the whole bus erupted in yells and abuse, the jeers accompanied by kicking of partitions, hammering of doors.

'Quiet!' white-shirt shouted as the van driver walked the length of the galley, whacking each cubicle door with a truncheon.

'Shut it, I said,' white-shirt snapped. 'Anyone up for murder or rape, speak now or God help you when we get inside.'

I heard someone near the back of the sweat wagon call, 'Me, guv' and the driver hurried over and unlocked the cubicle. I looked out through the cross-hatched grating of my cubicle in fascination as a pock-faced curly haired man was manhandled towards the front of the wagon by the driver. Once more the whole bus exploded into a clamour of thumping and shouts as the prisoner was taken across the floodlit forecourt towards the building.

The driver then began to work his way up the galley, unlocking the cubicles one by one. The prisoners left the bus and filed in through the main door of the remand centre to one side of which was a sign marked 'Reception'. When it was my turn I followed the others into the reception unit, a dimly lit room along one end of which was a wooden counter. I stood before this and a gruff old screw ordered me to strip. I slowly removed my clothes and watch and stood naked and shivering while a couple of leering prisoners packed my rags away in a cardboard box. Then it was a bath – the first I'd had in weeks – and I changed into a pair of grey trousers, a loose-fitting vest stamped with a blue crown and a blue and white striped shirt. I was given a clean towel, a bar of white soap, a comb and a pair of plastic slip-on shoes, which thankfully fitted me well. I got dressed and was told to wait in an overheated room that reminded me of the changing rooms we'd had at school. Wooden benches lined three sides and the ceiling was yellow and cracked. A barred window high in one of the walls granted me a view of the remand centre's fence and nothing more.

I was surprised to find that the other prisoners had already been led off to their cells and that I was now all alone. It turned out that this was because I was the only new arrival in my batch and had to have a medical. When the prison doctor arrived – a psychopathic-looking individual wearing half-moon glasses – I was shown to a little room, weighed, had my chest tapped with a stethoscope and was asked what drugs I was using. The doctor coughed quietly as he filled in some forms and placed them in a Manila folder already marked with my name. Then I was taken back to the waiting room. After half an hour an orderly brought me a meal – a ball of sticky white rice and a green curry sauce. When I'd eaten I was escorted by a screw down a long corridor along each side of which were rows of cell doors. We came to a steel gate behind which I saw a stair-case. The screw unlocked the gate and we climbed upwards floor by floor into the upper levels of the building. When we reached the fifth floor the screw unlocked another gate and led me down another corridor. He told me that we were in H wing and that it was considered to be the top security unit of the remand centre. I didn't know whether to feel horrified or proud on hearing this. Finally we came to an open cell door and I was ordered to enter. I did as I was told and passed through to dead crows hanging on coils of razor wire, dark shadowy wings on blasted moors. And I passed through to shreds of dried tobacco, the joy of books, O levels attained in education blocks, a sort of knowledge sometimes useful since.

SCARP'S DECLINE

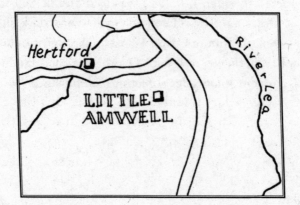

I STOOD BARE-HEADED IN THE churchyard at Little Berkhamsted and watched the raindrops bounce off Reginald Maudling's gravestone and drop into the soaked earth beneath. I longed to follow them. I was already down there somewhere anyway, being in essence nothing more than a momentary configuration of the soil. I felt ready any time to be wrapped in my tarpaulin and buried amidst these pebbles, the cloying brown clay.

I moved on up Robins Nest Hill past the rectory with its old garden walls bulging outwards over the pavement, to Stratton's Folly, a one hundred-foot red-brick tower built in 1789 as an observatory for John Stratton, a retired admiral. As I looked up at the castellated roof I thought about my previous visits to this place. One occasion in particular remained in my memory, a walk from Cuffley that led through Little Berkhamsted and on, across the Lea to Knebworth during the heatwave of the summer of 1998.

That day the whole of Hertfordshire had seemed a shimmering blinding plain of wheat. I'd ended up spending the night exhausted and dehydrated by the side of a disused farm track just off Bragbury Lane, near Stevenage, where, so the story goes, the Virgin Mary is said to walk every Lady's Day.

Waking the next morning exhausted and broke, I'd been overwhelmed by feelings of loneliness. I began to wonder whether it was all worth it, this solitary traipsing along lanes and paths that all began to look like each other after a while. I asked myself why it was I felt the need to go surging across the land, only to end curled up alone under discarded horse blankets in sealed-off feed roads or in the long grass behind bus shelters. What was it I was looking for out there? Day after day that summer I'd probed out from Borehamwood or Barnet or Pinner, sometimes walking as far north as the margins of the Great Midland Plain. Was it a person or presence I was seeking out on these walks, some of which lasted two or three days? I frequently felt, as I laid down my bag and spread my jacket on the ground in preparation for sleep each evening, that somebody hovered close by, a person who'd recently passed that way and left some trace of themselves lingering in the darkening trees. On other occasions, coming off pitch black hills down onto the lit streets of market towns, I sensed that she was out there somewhere in the endless streams of car lights.

Later, after I'd made it home and had a bath and a coffee, something deeper than my personal concerns rose in my mind. As I sat in my study staring at the pictorial map of Hertfordshire included in *The English Counties Illustrated*, with its inset illustrations of the Odhams Works at Watford and the BBC transmitters at Brookmans Park, I felt growing in me a pulsating county consciousness. I could sense sun-heated scraps of corrugated iron beneath which adders sheltered, bin-liners of rags strewn in wastes by remorseless A roads, scentless mayweed on gravel mounds nodding in the breeze by wretched abandoned orchards, languid afternoons spent sitting and sipping white wine in the gardens of big houses on the edge of the Hertfordshire atom towns, generations of owls and cats ruthlessly terminated by strychnine. I became a squirming energy spewing forth rats and roaches, disused fire extinguishers rusting in derelict office blocks in Hemel Hempstead or Stevenage. I roared, a fiery demiurge, below the pantiled bungalows, the pubs decked out in brewer's Tudor, throwing all this multiplicity into the world in my fury before subsiding back into the humming darkness of the undifferentiated planetary mass.

The silver disc of the sun sank lower behind the trees as I stared up at the battlements of Stratton's Folly. Shrugging off the weird memories of a day now more than ten years distant, I set off along Bucks Alley and downhill along a footpath to where the Bayford Brook cut through some drear woods.

Finally I reached the small village of Bayford where I caught the train back to Finsbury Park and then the tube home.

Two days later I took the Hertford train from Finsbury Park, intending to trace the high ground marked in brown on my *Bartholomew's One Inch Map of London's Roads and Countryside* from Bayford as far to the east as possible. I'd decided to find the end of Scarp, the point at which this tormenting shifting thing that had haunted me for years finally subsided into flat earth. The map indicated that the high ground receded in the vicinity of Little Amwell, originally the source of Hugh Myddelton's New River, which at one time provided London with most of its fresh water. As I sat, staring out the train window to the west I saw Alexandra Palace standing high and proud on its segment of London's northern heights. Shortly afterward the spire of Southgate's All Saints church appeared, a beckoning finger poking above the welt of suburbia surrounding it. Later there were other indications of Scarp's rumblings: a veering upwards and away of the streets at Bush Hill Park, near Enfield, the rows of houses ending at the wooded and rounded edges of the Crewes and Gordon Hills.

Specks of rain hit the train window as it crossed over the Northaw Brook at Sopers Viaduct. Off to the left ran the fields and hedges of Enfield Chase before climbing to high ground at Plumridge and Potters Bar. I sat and watched the dead banks of herbage, the stripped trees dopplering alongside the track and later caught a glimpse of a hunched, lean-faced old fox loping along the fence at the bottom of the railway embankment. It was cold out there, on the barren and flinty surface of the green belt.

The train entered the Ponsbourne Tunnel, which runs below the high ground I was intent on visiting that day, and then surfaced in the deep cutting at Bayford. I walked uphill from the station and turned to the left before reaching the village, heading south along an undulating cinder track. Despite it being only early afternoon, the sun was already low in the sky and its light, reflecting off the twin bands of track surface flattened by tractor tyres, worried my eyes.

To the left there was a plantation of young sessile oaks, and to the right, hornbeams. Fresh shoots of fool's parsley grew by the edge of the track and there were domes of comfrey amidst the rotting logs that lined the route. Colonies of the russet-coloured mushroom *Clitocybe infundibuliformis*, looking like wind-wrecked umbrellas, grew from tree stumps and at one point I passed a decrepit old farm gate along the top of which sprang the brittle antler-like grey sporophores of *Xylosphaera hypoxylon*.

The track swerved to the right at a farmhouse and worked its way round Blackfan Wood. I came out on White Stubbs Lane, a mere B road where, keeping an eye out for speeding cars, I aimed eastwards, intending to take a fieldpath further on to the village of Brickendon. The road dropped to a tributary of the Bayford Brook, which it crossed via a brick bridge and then rose again onto a dome of land beneath which, my map informed me, the railway tunnel ran. There was an airshaft in a field to the left, a grey brick cylinder around the top of which ran strands of barbed wire mounted on rusted saw-toothed spikes. A herd of cows clustered in the field's corner, sheltering from the cold wind.

It began to hail as I turned north along the track to Brickendon where I sought shelter in the church of St Mary, an austere timbered affair built in the 1930s to serve the village. I love this wooden-floored sanctuary with its neo-classical bas-relief inside the porch, its iron candelabras hanging from the ceiling and its window views across the Lea to belts of high ground far to the north. Looking out, I could see the white drum of the water tower at the Lister Hospital in Stevenage, some ten miles distant.

The hail stopped and I left Brickendon to cut eastwards again through damp, midge-infested sheep country, stepping cautiously over electric fences all the way to Monks Green Farm and then north onto a winding narrow road. I was definitely moving in the right direction: ahead, I could see the surface of the land dropping down to the river valley, the course of which could be traced by curving lines of trees and clusters of facto-ries built on the flood plain. I turned to the right, moving east-wards past old barns and a curious clock tower mounted on a hexagonal plastered plinth at Highfield Farm. Finally I arrived at a bridle path which cut directly across my route, heading uphill towards Little Amwell.

The high ground began to narrow towards a spur. To the north, east and north-west I had a clear view of the heights on the north bank of the Lea and the southern margins of the north-east Hertfordshire plateau. I passed a jack-head reservoir, indicating that I was on a local high spot, and entered a patch of woodland thick with holly and birch. Little Amwell's northern rim is formed by Mount Pleasant, a broad lane that curves around the crest of the outcrop on which the village is built. The road is lined with houses that are, for the most part, older than is the norm in the area and a late-nineteenth-century school building, now converted into flats. Further along there was an old inn – The Goat – and a triangular green with roads splitting off in several directions. Signs exhorted the locals not to leave litter or park on the green under threat of a fine. Looking back I saw the narrow spire of the church of Holy Trinity silhouetted against the umber of the evening sky.

Excitement grew in me at the prospect of discovering a precise location that I could declare to be Scarp's terminus. I set off along a road that dropped down towards the land below. I could see long chains of car lights at the bottom of the hill. Large flocks of crows gathered overhead before flying off to roost for the night. Ahead somewhere lay the town of Ware and the complex intertwining of the Lea Valley and the New River. This narrowing convex tongue of land subsiding down into the river valley felt like a finale.

As I reached the T-junction at the bottom of the road and looked back at the now distant church spire still silhouetted by the dying light, I felt exhilarated. Here, by this scrappy triangular traffic island and row of steel road-markers inset with red reflector panels, is where Scarp ends I declared.

The following day I returned, against my better judgement, back to Hertford Heath, intent merely on getting the maximum mileage out of my six-month travel pass, which was due to run out the next day. Besides, I felt that the culmination of my project warranted more than a single visit. This time I took a train north from Liverpool Street, along the Lea Valley. The sense of triumph I'd felt the previous day had evaporated. I felt ill and old; my head ached, my thoughts diffused; I wondered what it was I was trying to achieve. Looking out at the landscape I even doubted Scarp's existence.

The train crossed the narrow causeway between the Warwick reservoirs at Tottenham Hale. Edmonton Green passed, with its monolithic tower blocks, and then the acres of blue corrugated industrial units, their entrances screened by fringed transparent fire-curtains, at Brimsdown. I saw discarded sections of cable conduiting dumped in the long grass by the trackside and sections of wire fencing mounted on concrete plinths slowly sinking into oceans of bramble, having been usurped by spiked rustproof palings.

I arrived at St Margarets, the next town down the line from Ware, where I'd caught the train back to London the day before. My aim was to approach Little Amwell from the east, hitting the ridgeline sideways on. Walking out of the station I aimed due west along a busy B road. Soon I left the houses behind me, the road running through fields on either side. Far to the south I saw a long sunlit ridge etched with field lines. For an awful moment I feared that it was some offshoot of Scarp that I'd somehow overlooked, but soon came to the conclusion that I was in fact looking at the heights around Nazeing in Essex, on the far side of the Lea.

Ahead of me I saw black woodlands peering over a compacted wedge of modern suburbia tucked between two sweeping main roads. By the time I reached Amwell Roundabout there was no doubting the presence of the high land – this was what I'd come here for.

Then it was uphill along a broad track between lines of coppiced hornbeams. There were thick carpets of oak leaves everywhere and a moss-capped embankment to the left, presumably an old boundary. Finally, I arrived back at Mount Pleasant and visited The Goat for sausages and mash.

Everything had been stripped of the veneer it had possessed the previous day. I noticed a pair of workmen were delivering a Christmas tree to the thin-spired church and I took the opportunity to follow them inside. Staring blankly at the plastered interior walls, the artfully patterned brickwork I realised I had no grasp whatsoever of church architecture. In fact, I felt as if I'd learnt next to nothing about anything I'd seen over all the years I'd been walking.

I planned to drop off the north-western edge of the high ground around Little Amwell and walk down into Hertford. It was all part of feeling out the area. I followed narrow Vicarage Causeway onto London Road and into a field that led downhill to a brook and the piggery at Foxholes Farm. After crossing the farmyard I passed into a tunnel below the A10 and emerged onto a patch of rough parkland with the roofs of factories poking above the treeline to the left. Ahead, perched oddly on a set of steeply pitched roadways, were lines of 1930s houses, their familiar curved window frames a welcome sight after all the solitude, all the emptiness of the afternoon. It grew colder and I felt defeated by Scarp. Looking back on the way I'd just come I had no sense of the pristine and pure diminuendo I had experienced the previous day. All I could see was a confusing mass of mounds and pinnacles visible beyond the semi-detacheds at the town's edge. Somewhere in my dulled mind I knew that this was as it should be: Scarp should remain an evasive entity that twisted out of my understanding, slipping free of any notion I had of gaining mastery over it.

Hertford seemed particularly cheerless that afternoon. As I headed west along the Ware Road I once again found myself wondering what all the walking undertaken over the past few years had actually given me. I passed the art-deco Addis toothbrush factory – now the print works for the *Essex and Hertfordshire Press* – and turned down Mill Road for Hertford East Station. A cup of tea and an illicit fag helped pass the twenty-minute wait for the train. Rain hissed on the station roof and gangs of screaming schoolkids crowded the platform. Finally the train arrived and I clambered aboard. Moments later, accompanied by a whistle from the aged and grey-whiskered stationmaster, the train pulled off along the floor of the Lea Valley towards Ware and on to London.

Then I noticed something that had eluded me during all my endless map studies. The train was rushing through a broad flood plain intersected with channels and ditches. Large patches of dead marsh thistle, teasel and mugwort stretched away on either side. As the train came out from under the viaduct carrying the A10 over the river valley, I glanced out of the window at the Hertford suburb of Pinehurst with its houses set in neat tiers along the side of an unexpectedly steep ridge. And there, overlooking the uppermost rooftops I saw a dark embankment formed of solid earth topped by dense masses of winter trees. As I stared upwards, both horrified and exhilarated, Scarp raised its bony fingers to claw the blank winter sky and gazed back down on me and through me into deeper time.

*

Merops flaps, a frayed scrap of sky-stuff, through ever thickening air. Then he holds his wingtips steady and glides across the traffic lanes, under the fizzing power cables. The clouds are hanging heavy and threaten to release a belly full of rain as a deep darkness builds in the west. A 747 rising from Heathrow climbs overhead, the scream of its engines shaking the windows of the motels along the A41, loosening the particles of soil packed around Philippa Gordon, resting in her grave on Sandy Lane.

Gloria, Queen of the PAMS, vanilla-scented and still alive despite the odds, her hair hennaed and plaited, picks her way between patches of iron-browned water and tufts of moor grass, keeping where possible to the driest tussocks. She begins her ascent out of the Colne Valley at Hamper Mill, and climbs to Moor Park where the caddies stand around smoking in the sun. She has made her decision and is ready now to try a new mode of life, this bounded by the chintzy furnishings, panelled studies and old stuffed armchairs of her evolving imagination.

John Osborne has been caught scattering nails onto the northbound lane of the A10 near Amwell Roundabout. As this reeking straw-stuffed scarecrow of defeat is led off to a waiting police van he looks down at the corpse of a badger clipped by a passing car shortly before. One of the arresting officers lifts the inert bag of fur and claws over with his boot and it tumbles down the motorway embankment into a bed of wormwood and nettles. The badger's face – a mint humbug with teeth and tuberculosis – stares up at them from its final resting place.

As for me, I have to stop and sit to catch my breath. Hot and sweaty beneath my bright orange cagoule I roll a fag and take the time to survey the lands below. A bead curtain of rain advances up the slope and hits me full-on. I pull my hood up over my prickling scalp and stare mindlessly at the view – another nameless blob of new housing squeezed into the space between the more obstinate landscape features – and wonder what justice I could do this protracted sequence of exposures to Scarp. Will I write hill poetry, like some eighteenth-century parson with a literary bent? Will I come on all nineteenth-century aesthete with my silk smoking jacket and cravat, dedicating these clusters of words, fragments of a larger, unwritten work, to some pale-skinned princess of the echoing hills?

And Scarp? It licks me all over in preparation for its feast. It speaks to me in all its many tongues, even as it slowly skins me alive. It is this soft blue feather I saw spinning down from the oak where a sparrow hawk perched briefly and I now place between the pages of my notebook. It is the moment a sprinter just out of Potters Bar thrusts through the cutting north of Wagon Lane before disappearing into the tunnel leading to Hadley Station. It is the wolf spider I saw running across a piece of damp paper snagged in a barbed-wire fence near Essendon or the giblets of a torn pigeon scattered amidst the smashed porcelain in the ruins of a public lavatory by the A41. I turn again and again to face this half-imagined sequence of places, each time fooling myself into thinking I've gained mastery over it, but always Scarp wrenches itself from my grasp, stealing a march on me before settling down somewhere ahead in ambush.

Merops watches the cars and trucks from his vantage point, the roof of a travellers' caravan, just one among many mounted on brick foundations by Gullimore Farm. As the London-bound traffic drearily passes he thinks once again of this domain of his and of what has transpired and what will be. Once, not so far back, the Town & Country Planning Act sat on the map. Now there are plans for high-speed railway lines cutting through Harefield, green wedges replacing broader tracts of farm country and ever-expanding pockets of affordable housing edging in on his province. He feels low and tired of it all, knowing the inevitability of change, something he had once welcomed but now no longer relishes. There is a momentary pause in the traffic and, drawn out of himself by the relative quiet, Merops watches as a small grey squirrel bounds in panic out into the road, trying to escape some unseen threat. Now the next block of traffic is closing fast and the squirrel freezes in terror, unable to do anything other than stare directly into the face of the cars roaring towards it. The first vehicle gives the squirrel a glancing blow, knocking it sideways into the next lane. To Merops' surprise the small animal is still alive and runs round in small circles as intestines pullulate from a large rip in its stomach. A second later and it's all over – a van whips past, in an instant reducing the helpless creature to a wind-twitched and red-stained patch of grey fur flush with the road surface.

Gloria Geddes stands beside the eighteenth-century club-house, turns and faces north, looking towards Croxley on the far side of the Colne Valley. She can sense the intimate details of the lives lived out in the distant villas and bungalows visible on the hillside. One house in particular holds her attention, a four-square semi-detached in the denuded garden of which (she imagines) there ticks a warm-engined Mercedes or BMW. Is it *his* life, the home kept by Raggadagga and *that woman* she sees in her mind? She braces herself for the familiar pain but to her surprise it doesn't come: another, a new Raggadagga, is waiting for her somewhere, perhaps hidden in that patch of broom growing near the pond, just by where the track crosses the 14th tee and drops to rumours of a Roman villa. She breathes deeply and watches a golfer trundle his Burberry golf bag past the 15th hole.

John Osborne mutters away to himself as he's led down the hospital corridor by two officers from the Hertfordshire Constabulary. He's delaying his escape 'just to see what happens'. Besides, he's hungry and the smell of stew and pota-toes seeping out from under the double doors of the locked dining room at the end of the corridor holds him. Just long enough to fill my belly and I'm off and out of this piss-hole, he thinks. He's led through the doors and the coppers hand him over to a hospital worker who tells him to sit and wait to be seen by the doctor. A large TV mounted on the wall casts its flickering light on a group of patients seated in the corner of the room. One of them leans forward, half-comatose, spittle dangling in strings from his protruding lips. An angry young woman with vicious eyes twirls her fingers through her hair. Another patient – a bearded man with a filthy-looking thatch of dreadlocks piled above his creviced face – rocks backwards and forwards mumbling to himself. Bollocks to this, John Osborne thinks as he pulls a plastic orange chair from the stack by the wall and settles down with a paper to study form.

'Mind if I smoke?' he asks the Barbadian charge nurse sitting in the glass-windowed office at the room's far end.

'No smoking, darling,' she replies. 'You'll have to wait till the doctor's seen you and then we'll let you outside.'

Sod it, he thinks. A meal and I'm skedaddling back to my hedge life, my field wandering. They won't miss me. Another ten years' fast-forwarding and there'll be nothing left of this shower anyway.

I sit in the barn at Colesdale Farm, having sneaked across the cobbled yard past a hand busily engaged in filling a kettle from a tap mounted in the wall of the farmhouse. I enter the pigeon-infested darkness, the spiderwebs hanging from rafters, and climb onto the stacked hay bales. I will sleep here, my thoughts spiralling out over the land as I drift off.

Gloria savours the early flowers, the brook set deep in its sandy gulley, the sound of hammers ringing from the clubhouse as the winter damage is repaired and the springtime optimism evident in the small talk of golfers standing in groups by the Scotch pines. Soon she will make her move, will join this cosy, comfortable world of certainties. She can already hear the jaguar crunching on the gravel drive, taste the fine wine thrilling her throat, and see the terraced bed of alpines as she peers through mullioned windows.

I drift off and phase into blustering air-movement above Scarp. Great flaps of wind slap my face as I circle over the green girdle. I fade to past summers and lost opportunities. I freeze to concrete patterning on post-war shopfronts in Watford and Elstree. The years – curled and yellow – peel off from the Great Book before blowing away to nothingness. Finally, I sleep.

Merops makes his decision and drops heavily down to the steaming fresh roadkill. As he bends forward, the better to sniff out the tenderised offal, to pick at the oozing guts, an articulated truck transporting aggregate from Bedfordshire for some new building development down south flattens him. Then the lorry has passed and all that remains of Merops is a blood-matted quiver poking from the pottage smeared across the road.

The moment is ripe, Gloria thinks as she approaches a club member shagging for his ball in the herbage. My name will be etched on trophies displayed in glass-fronted cabinets, she muses. I will be a listed member in club-committee minutes. I will slowly knock back G&Ts, become an organiser of charity quizzes. She moves in closer and the golfer looks up, startled by her approach. Closing in on him now, Gloria lifts her skirt and, stepping forward, presses her warmth to the golfer's milling mouth.

John Osborne sighs, folds the newspaper and rises to leave, heading towards the door to the dining room; he is missing the fields, the belts of hawthorn edging the M1, and can hardly breathe in this TV-polluted, drugged-up and drooling room. A muscular psychiatric nurse wearing ironed jeans and a white T-shirt appears, seemingly from nowhere and moves swiftly to block his exit.

'Sorry mate, you can't go out,' he says, the look on his unreasonably healthy face managing to convey community care and menace in one go.

'Listen, sunshine, I could slip through that keyhole. I could kill you anytime I like, so be a good boy and let me leave,' John growls, his voice conveying all the ancient authority of the tree-twisted, weed-tangled, ditch-watered landscape lying in wait beyond the hospital's confines.

'The doctor needs to see you first,' the nurse replies firmly, not giving an inch. He is joined by two Africans dressed in matching loose-fitting smocks and trousers. All three of them stare at him, seemingly daring him to make a move.

'Now, sit down over there and watch TV please,' the nurse continues as his colleagues move in on either side, ready to grab John Osborne's arms, should he decide to kick off.

With a despondent sigh he sits and smacks the rolled paper against the Formica-topped table before opening it again. It's no real problem – come the night he'll spirit himself out of this place and then there'll be a hoo-ha in the nursing station. Then they'll see who they're dealing with. He smiles to himself and settles down to read, as he was taught to do back in 1709.

I wake in a panic in the dark barn and gather my map and compass, my tobacco tin in preparation for leaving. A sense that something has been sheared off from the land and has slipped over the event horizon leaves me unsettled as I head off towards the nearest railway station. It is mid-November now and the late autumn has crept up on me. The darkness descends and map reading becomes impossible. Still, it has its compensations. There is poetry in the lit windows of the town that is my destination, a sense of movement and life in people heading for warm homes. As the walk levels out and I hit a small municipal park, I sit down to eat my hummus and spin-ach sandwiches and jot down my observations in a notebook. I smoke as I write; the scent of tobacco mingling with the smell of mould drifting from the leaves swept up and piled in the gutter.

A flesh fly appears out of the encroaching darkness and lands on my knee. My attempt to brush it back into flight provokes no response. Something is up with it. I watch it closely as it cleans itself, its front legs rubbing its face despondently. This tiny speck of life left washed up and alone by its given season reverses slightly and shifts its facing as the darkness around us increases and the last commuters disappear into the gloom. A cold blast ruffles the grass and the fly shifts again, its wings whirring furiously, but there is no flight. Once again I move to brush it off but the fly merely sits there, seemingly staring at the flickering car lights. Finally, a gust lifts it from my knee and it tumbles onto the pathway and skates along on its back in the breeze before settling on the concrete. With a last desperate buzz it manages to flip over and I watch horrified as it rocks gently on the keel of its locked legs. The evening wind rises again and the dead fly tumbles away until it disappears somewhere in the grass. Blackness descends on all the land and, as Scarp shadows me, a burden draped heavily around my shoulders, I pack away my maps and notebook, rise, and walk on.

APPENDIX

PERRY KURLAND'S JOURNAL

20 III 74
Brandy Bottles
Stinking Jenny
Ramsons[1]

There is a purple and brown pigeon nesting in my gutter, a rook on the chimney of the house by the alley as I leave this morning. Large spotted leaves (I thought they were lungwort) are growing by the old ruined church tower at Stanmore. They look juicy & plump, rather like comfrey. I suspect they are green alkanet – rare in these parts.[2]

This isn't some TV-series or drama-workshop universe. This is the real world, Sir: the realm of ants swarming on kerbstones and wasps tapping against the window at dawn. There are sandy mounds behind the brake-drum factory; a myriad of insects dying in drainage ditches or under wheels. They click in

1 *Brandy Bottles* etc: folk names for *Allium ursinum* L, broad-leaved garlic.
2 In fact, *Pentaglottis sempervirens* L, green alkanet, was already extremely common 'in these parts' by 1974. However, according to *British Herbs*, Florence Ranson, Pelican 1949, the plant was, at *that* time, 'rare outside of coastal areas'.

their death throes as they are torn by mandibles, stamped on by children, squashed under tyres by roadside verge. The world is a fiery storm roaring at the base of the hedge – flames spreading, invisible in the tussocks.

When I leave my front door and walk, say, ten miles in any direction, I see <u>the world</u>. I see <u>what is there</u>: the ruins of failed companies, their letterboxes clogged with circulars and final demands unread; smoke-blackened boxing clubs above stinking shopfronts fitted with sodden carpets; deep vacuum Y-front people in numbers beyond any mind to grasp.

Proceed and there is sheep's sorrel waving by traffic queues. Here it ends, at coltsfoot outside MacFisheries[3] and mineral dust spiralling from hot, cracked pavements.

It is at these times – my eyes opening onto the hallways of lives lived in silence – that I have a clear memory of <u>her</u> departure – duffel coat flapping – a momentary trace amidst multiple compressions.[4]

---

3 *MacFisheries*: High-street chain specialising in frozen and canned goods; defunct by late 1970s.

4 *Her*: Kurland makes occasional reference to a female presence in this journal. It would seem to have not been his wife, Annette. Whether the reference is to a former lover or an entirely imaginary person is unclear.

22 III 74

Cocky Baby
Dog's Dibble
Devil's Men & Women[5]

Buying numerous books recently – The Deep Library. There is rain on the window as the codeine bites. I am on the hills west of Bayford, 1929. I am trackways and field paths. I become a beehive, the pulsing of a wasp's abdomen. I am a field of wheat, red seeds of wild parsnip.

In the market towns the cattle are packed, bewildered. I drink ale amidst the stench of bull's dung and tobacco.

1 IV 74

Little Nathan Allenstein sat down and waited. I no longer wish to waste time grooming these Levantine curls, these nebulae spiralling out to a life spent in Carpenders Park or Edgwarebury. Instead I tonsure the future world – snip-snip – and a universe dies. I desire a walk and the meadows, the concrete paths, summon me. This p.m. I was frog-marched, drunk, out of my own salon,[6] my berewick. Annette was furious and I'm banished from the curtained room, the hot fish, so I climb the stairs to my study.

5 *Cocky Baby* etc: folk names for *Arum maculatum* L, wild arum.
6 *Salon*: Kurland owned and managed the My Fair Lady hair salon in Mill Hill Broadway until his untimely death in 1978.

3 IV 74

Pompidou dies! QE2 crippled! It is all <u>Chigley</u>, all <u>Nai Zindagi</u>, <u>Nai Jeevah</u>[7] and Annette weeping in front of the daytime gogglebox. I'm off and out, Stanmore to Love Lane, Pinner.

Up the hill above Ruislip, then slipping down through Mad Bess[8] and out, over to windy Harefield. Drop down across canal, by gravel pits, and up the other side of the Colne Valley along Old Shire Lane. There is a snagged tree and stitchwort wobbles in the sad grass. A fifty-yd. turn left and up again, ahead to Chorley Wood. Here, where the lip of the hill points NNW, the lights of a distant car rising, rising, into the dark unknown.

7 IV 74

Clatterclogs
Dummy-Weed
Tushy-Lucky Gowan[9]

Ask the banner-waving vegetarians, the Eastcote esotericists, where their number twos goes. 'Into the sewers, of course,' they invariably reply, but where precisely? I ponder this question frequently. To answer this we need to consider the rivers and streams of our region, for the engineers who build our

---

7 *Chigley*; *Nai Zindagi, Nai Jeevah*: TV programmes from the 1970s.
8 *Mad Bess*: Mad Bess Wood, near Ruislip.
9 *Clatterclogs* etc: folk names for *Tussilago farfara* L, coltsfoot.

systems of disposal will always base the orientation of their sewers upon pre-existing watercourses to assure flow. They examine the precise points of discharge off the watersheds and align their tubing accordingly.

These simulacra of the natural watercourses fascinate me. They run disregarded under our crowded high streets, below the oft-overlooked accommodation roads at the back of 1930s' shopping parades, beneath alleyways, between houses. These are our modern ley lines; purposive channels of energy embedded in the landscape and marked by their own forms of tumulus and standing stone.

I spent yesterday walking to Watford via Bushey and slept overnight in the darkness and safety of Cassiobury Park. Today I follow the old railway line to Rickmansworth and wander through the new shopping and leisure complex. I lurch past the bananas and stacked stereophonic radiograms and out to the footpath along the Colne.

On the scent now, I wind along the stream opposite walled substations. The town smudges out at new estates and solitary pylons. A silence descends and there is a sense of being on the rim of the imprinted city. Ahead are outliers of the Chiltern range and the peculiarities of Bucks, but that is another world.

I head south to a junction at Maple Grove Farm. Taking the road to the left, I edge down by iron bridges spanning ditches and weed-packed spaces wedged between narrow gauge railways and council depots. These are the ancillary margins of the Colne towns, frequented by stray woodpeckers and myopic ornithologists. As the road curves over another bridge towards the left, a set of blue gates appears up ahead. I can go no further and must gaze through the fence and past the prefab security hut. The view is of a straight track, edged by granolithic reservoirs and off-white methane tanks. Gulls wheel over aeration lagoons. A windsock hangs limply by blue-railed steps. These lead down to a powerhouse with a glass-brick doorway. At the track's terminus a low concrete block stands, as I always knew it would. The circuit is complete: I confront my disowned self. Here is the utile place, squat and sinister: journey's end.[10]

1 V 74
Spink
Moll Blobs
Lamb's Lakens[11]

Annette went off to see Jeremy Thorpe in Harrow. I drop her at the station and drive to North Harrow. Walk down the Yeading brook via Northolt to confluence with Roxbourne. Brick structure topped with plate:

MIDDLESEX/COUNTY/COUNCIL/1934

A naked man sits on a blanket in the long grass, smoking.

10 This seems to be a depiction of the Maple Cross sewage farm, the terminal treatment works for the West Hertfordshire Main Drainage Scheme.
11 *Spink* etc: folk names for *Cardamine pratensis* L, Lady's Smock.

For a second I think it is Grzegoz.[12] He scowls as I pass. Later I see the curving rails of GWR in sunset; the blue of the Southall gasometer. I end at Isleworth: stench of sewage.

This issue with Anne Aston[13] is getting out of hand. She lost her engagement ring while visiting my salon and says it was worth six hundred pounds. That's more than I earn in a month.

Permanently hot to trot and fresh from flashing her cleavage on <u>The Golden Shot</u>,[14] doesn't she have enough already?

11 V 74
Bad Man's Oatmeal
Tacker Weed
Pick-Your-Mother's-Eyes-Out[15]

Deep Topography is concerned primarily with the <u>experience</u> of place, <u>not</u> its description. However, it is recognised that a complex and mutually reinforcing relationship exists between these two categories.

Deep Topography: a duty to explore.

12 *Grzegorz*: Grzegorz Morderca (1897–1979), Polish émigré poet resident in the Hendon area.
13 *Anne Aston*: Actress and television presenter best known as the hostess of *The Golden Shot* in the late 1960s and early 1970s.
14 *The Golden Shot*: a popular TV quiz show from the early 1970s.
15 *Bad Man's Oatmeal* etc: folk names for *Capsella bursa-pastoris* L, Shepherd's Purse.

Deep Topography is <u>not</u> a problem-solving approach to the world, if that concept is defined purely in terms of increasing or improving degree of instrumentality.

Deep Topography places an emphasis on found items – lists dropped on pavements; letters found in attics of condemned houses; personal papers discarded in skips.

It is difficult to place parameters on what constitutes Deep Topographic inquiry: any formula generated for purposes of cultural elucidation – even the one expressed in this sentence – interferes with the procedure.

Deep Topography: pieces of rusted machinery stumbled upon in dry grasses by Grim's Dyke, 1967; a box of telephone components found on Enfield Chase during an undated summer about twenty-three years ago: spread the parts out on the table and try to work out the relations between them.

Deep Topography is a dip down into the valley of the unacknowledged: Suicide Corner, June 1958.[16]

Deep Topography is a transmission across time, confounding the thought that all has been swept away: the Allenstein bird table, 1961–1972.

The accusation of nostalgia could reasonably be levelled at Deep Topography. However, that sentiment is attained not through absence from one's home but via passing through the land's eye.

---

16 *Suicide Corner*: The only Suicide Corner I am aware of is marked as such on my 1962 edition of *Bartholomew's Reference Atlas of Greater London*; it is the name given for the junction of the A41 with the A5 high on the North Middlesex Tertiary Escarpment.

Deep Topography: a return to home at day's end and, after the exhaustion, a rising into something that is more than personal recollection: rather, it is the land's very structure and memory unfurling in the mind.

19 V 74
Fleas and Lice
Mother of Millions
Nanny Goat's Mouth[17]

Anxiety and tears: Maalot and Dublin.[18] The Dead continues to cluster! I sicken at this life, at Annette's demands. She insists the new car must have an 'aerodynamic spoiler', wants our funds transferred to this newfangled Leicester Building Society. I have other concerns on my mind.

Following last month's little 'problem' I realise I'm too dispersed. I solemnly resolve to pursue the following cleansing regime:

1. To abstain completely from all vehicular transport. This to include bicycle and bus (red or green).
2. To restrict all movement to within the Hundred of Gore for a period not less than, and not exceeding six months.[19]

17 *Fleas and Lice* etc: folk names for *Cymbalaria muralis* Gaertner, Meyer & Scherbius, Ivy-leaved Toadflax.
18 *Maalot and Dublin*: contemporary locations of terrorist bomb outrages.
19 *Hundred of Gore*: an administrative area within the old County of

Blocked by a lost city to the north – tiles for Hadrian's wall; an ancient ditch running through laurel; electrical engineers.[20]

By tower blocks to the south – atrophied intent at buried rifle ranges.[21]

By synthetic village to the east – a border of bagshots and bankers.[22]

By the Hog's Back[23] to the west – it is a quick flick to devastation on the chalk mounds.

20 V 74

A dream: I am soft mush bubbling down to a turdy confluence; I trickle along concrete runnels through back gardens and pass window blinds and sheds packed with old paint tins and rusting bikes. I gurgle, mumble into dark while fed by flushings from

---

Middlesex. It would seem that Kurland fails to keep to this self-imposed stricture – within days he has journeyed out to Buckinghamshire!

20 *Blocked by a lost city to the north*: probably a reference to the Roman way station of Sulloniacae. This is generally taken to have been located at Stanmore (on the northern edge of the Hundred of Gore). There is an area of Stanmore named 'The City'.

21 *By tower blocks to the south*: Possibly the Granville Road estate on the border of London Boroughs of Barnet and Camden (on the southern edge of the Hundred of Gore).

22 *By synthetic village to the east*: Almost certainly Hampstead Garden suburb. Bagshot sands are found on Hampstead Heath, not far from the suburb.

23 *Hogs Back*: Kurland seems to be referring to the small park bearing the same name in Northwood, Middlesex, *not* the Hog's Back on the North Downs in Surrey.

pink lavatories, from tepid baths. I am the real town, Sir: flowing by weed-clad iron palings; under concrete lids and mounds
behind garages. Screened out for decency's sake by script-
writers, editors and other dealers in 'truth', I rush eastward
towards my fate and end in sediments and tomato plants at
Edmonton. I am rotated while waders pick my choicest solids
and am pumped fresh and born again into the New Cut.[24]

3 VI 74

There is a rushing of feet, a chaos of S-belts by foaming brooks.
The coach is in the coach-house, the Dalek in the post office.
Up Squire's Lane the imprint fades as the electricity tower is
erected by Hunter's allotment, 1960.

I see the curve of green roofs in Mother's apothecary jar.
I see 'goofy' American cartoons and olive-skinned detectives
chasing Russian spies.

But now the gate squeaks. Now they wear checked flares and
hush puppies. They sport drooping moustaches and sideburns:
'You've been a naughty man, Mr Kurland.'

We stored meths in the shed on Hunter's allotment.
The commerce block went up in flames. We kicked Gavin
in the balls by the foaming brook. Tucker was caught at
East Finchley and hauled to court at Highgate. It is the new
building (1954 – a rocket-bomb did for the old station in

---

24 *New Cut*: presumably a reference to the River Lea Navigation Canal
– the dream seems to be about sewage.

1944). All the Roman Road is grateful: Frigidaire; Clangs Cars; Spurling Motor Bodies; Rawlplug.[25] There is an unremitting production towards surplus. All agree to the Mogden Formula:[26]

$$C = R + V + V_b + B \times Ot/Os + S \times St/Ss$$

Where C = Total charge rate for disposal, pence/cubic metre. (The old lady living at Clive Court by the North Circular. It is 1934 and Constant Lambert plays on the radio. I'm driving past, riding the river valleys, Pymmes to Coles to Mutton to Brent. There is a small stream at the confluence, behind the pumping station at World's End.)

Where R = Unit cost for conveyance, pence/cubic metre. (The old lady taking a diesel bus out to a scattering of field-paths by the church of St Andrew's, Kingsbury. New rail lines slice into hay meadows. A moment's passing at eventide gives way to larger churches and blazing warehouses along the Watford Way.)

Where V = Unit cost for volumetric treatment, pence/cubic metre. (The old lady growing fat. Her ordure pumped to

25 *Frigidaire*; *Clangs Cars*; *Spurling Motor Bodies*; *Rawlplug*: regional manufactories. Most of these disappeared about the time the journal was written.

26 *Mogden Formula*: internationally recognised formula for estimating charges to industry for waste-disposal via sewage pipes. The formula is named after Mogden Purification Works in Isleworth, Middlesex, terminal of the West Middlesex Main Drainage Scheme.

Monk's Park. Flies with red compound eyes flick around the Wembley puddings.)[27]

Where V_b = Additional volume charge if there is no biological treatment. (The old lady falling down the stairs. *Brrrring! Brrrring!* She is taken to the North Middlesex Hospital.)

Where B = Unit cost for biological treatment, pence/cubic metre. (The old lady staying with her sister in Upper Barvin; pears and punnets of berries eaten in the shade.)

Where Ot = COD of trade effluent, mg/l; Os = COD settled sewage. (The old lady watching the Trident whistle out above Foxhole Hill. Scooters pass on the road between Enfield and Potters Bar.)

Where S = Unit cost for sludge disposal, pence/cubic metre. (The old lady stares at the rock 'n' roll letch as his leather-laced crotch splits live on the blue box.)

Where St = Solids value trade effluent, mg/l; Ss = Solids value settled sewage. (A useless death at Cuffley. The old lady is laid out on the steel table while the mortuary assistant eats curry – a ring of rice; coconut sprinklings; sultanas and cubes of beef.)

27 *Wembley Pudding*: end-result of groundbreaking treatment of sewage sludge developed at the old Wembley Urban District Council sewage works, Alperton, in the 1920s. The resulting cakes of dried waste were sold as fertiliser.

21 VI 74
Stingy-Wingies
Snuff-candle
Deaf and Dumb[28]

Grzegorz writes; sends his latest work, <u>The Aims of a Walker</u>, printed in smudged heavy ink, not on his Gestetner, as I'd expected, but with a vintage Banda rotary drum. Time travel in the green girdle seems to be the subject. He states nothing explicitly but it's all leading towards his obsession with the dissolution of the county of Middlesex. On top of that, I'm certain he's moving in on my interest in sewerage. This afternoon I visited the London Museum at Kensington Palace and was informed that somebody had filched the official brochure commemorating the opening of Mogden Purification Works (1936).

   Grzegorz with his mythic coastlines, his 'deep feeling' for Bobrowski's Sarmatia:[29] am I not the Baltic Prince, Kurland from Courland, with my memories of Memel, of Tilsit?

   Black swastikas, red stars: child of Mars, the red god of war.

---

28 *Stingy-Wingies* etc: folk names for *Galeobdolon luteum*, Hudson, Yellow Dead Nettle.
29 *Bobrowski's Sarmatia*: Johannes Bobrowski (1917–65), East German poet, whose collection *Sarmatische Zeit* (Sarmatian Time) influenced the work of Morderca.

3 VII 74

All night inside the Deep Library: humming to myself as I walk along the millrace and then departing by train in July 1914, never to return. I am the rat-catcher, a believer in the efficacy of bryony[30] the English mandrake wrapped in newspapers and hung in garden sheds in Bushey.

How to explain this Deep Library? It begins with the brothers <u>Brimble</u>;[31] moves on to the brothers <u>Maxwell</u>.[32] Then there was Sir Montagu Sharpe, one-time chairman of the RSPB and of the Middlesex County Council. He lived in the parish of Hanwell; attended the opening of Mogden sewage-treatment works.

These are my local gods: in <u>The Fringe of London</u> (1926) Donald S. Maxwell went in search of the village of Monk's Park, wanted to see this backwater, stuck with a rural postal service four miles from Marble Arch. In the south-east of the Hundred, home to the sons of Toka,[33] NCR, LBB.

A confluence behind the villas, in a no-man's-land between

---

30 *Bryony: Bryonia doica*, Jacq. Red bryony was considered at one time to be the *mandragoras* of the Greeks.

31 *Brothers Brimble*: probably a reference to L.J.F. Brimble, one-time editor of *Nature* and popular writer on wild plants and J.A. Brimble, author of *London's Epping Forest* (1952).

32 *Brothers Maxwell*: Gordon S. Maxwell and his brother, Donald produced a series of popular illustrated topographies in the 1920s and '30s including *The Fringe of London* (1926), *Highwayman's Heath* (1930) and *Unknown Sussex* (1925). Many of their books dealt with areas of Middlesex and Hertfordshire.

33 *Toka*: probably reference to Tokyngton, near Wembley, Middlesex.

factories – Lidding Brook seen momentarily from the Metropolitan Railway.

The gods waver and fade to coffee bars. Where Slade Brook slops under the Raphael estate and runs into the river Brent while the canal feeder flows beneath the NCR. Here the gods now reside, in rotting fences concealing discarded rolls of wallpaper, shattered cola bottles.

Path-finder and Fieldfare writing in the <u>Evening News</u>: in <u>Afoot Round London (North)</u> (c. 1913) Path-finder tracks through London's 'little Lakeland': Pinner–Batchworth Heath–Watford. I arrive back at Binyon Crescent in great exhaustion from the last-named. Collapsing to Camp Coffee and Woodbines I read Path-finder's account and am drawn beyond sodium light. I spread across the western county and plunge deep into Pinner's hidden chalk mines.

12 VII 74

Annette works day and night, seeking to repeat her hairstyling glory days. I have no taste for it and am off and out, north to other lands.

I come to a new suburb after walking the damp dark wood and, upon finding it, am staggered to think how lost we all are, not even knowing our own city.

It is where the neat and well-scrubbed private roads with their distinctive protracted camber drop down to a stream running eastwards into marshes. It is where the small Methodist chapel, with its cypresses and its benches dedicated to persons I will never know, has stood right here throughout my time on earth, yet has never declared itself.

Hence there is a throwness, a presence unmediated by habit, about the place on this storm-cloud threatened afternoon; a jutting-forth of these fine houses and shrubby traffic islands onto the surface of a planet whose name suddenly eludes me.

It is always like this when I stumble on the place-unknown just beyond the place-known. Starting out this afternoon at High Barnet – a town familiar to me since youth – I probed by edges of sports fields and crept through new estates. Up the hill, over the bridge and down by the oak saplings alongside the railway track. On a whim I turned left instead of right and came between villas to this strange place. It is at these times that the conditioned decades evaporate and a new, an urgent depth is attained.

I walked through to where homes of giddying wealth stand triumphantly in their own space. A little brook runs eastwards from off the glacial moraine. I'm dazzled and so out of place in this place I find it impossible to imagine the owners of these houses sharing any art, history or even bodily function with me.

I ask an old gentleman sitting by the church the name of the brook. He doesn't know. Later I find it is the Green Brook. The Green Brook! Has it waited long, this little stream whose course marks the boundary between the woods and this private estate? Has it really flowed patiently through all these years, hers and mine, through all our useless wars and governments? I follow this vital hermetic impulse buried by decades of junk and torpor down to where it disappears beneath Sewit's Hill.

Slowly the obdurate suburb yielded. I couldn't understand how a ten-minute walk down a dull-looking road took me from a suffocating high street known since birth to the windy lip of a hill and a view of endless roofs receding to clouds. Something terrifying hovered in the shifting spaces between the trees' leaf-dense branches. It whispered through the bending grass on the playing fields. Displacement can kill: displacement can cure. Both outcomes can feel frighteningly similar.

Here was the place I should always already have known. Through the latticed windows colour TV screens flickered in darkened rooms. A whole world enters rooms where I cannot go and intelligent faces discuss the fate of nations. Evening laps up against rolled lawns and barren flowerbeds and is swallowed by a sophisticated yawn.

The firs darken – aliens outlined against the fading sky – and a robin sings, his voice warming like a little campfire. A final light lingers at these times. There is something taut, something clean and sharp, like the facet of a diamond, suspended in the sky. A little day is claimed back from the dark tides of the gathering storm clouds' depths and the world begins to stock up for another grand offensive against entropy and death.

28 VII 74

Deep Library says follow Path-finder back to Denham Golf course. I'm out early and up at Uxbridge, bound to my mentor in his rambles, storming once again across the Colne, through meadows, along an alley at the back of council houses and out into a pylon-infested plain cut by the little Alderbourne.

There is a screaming by complexities of railways; a small bridge leads to blobs of bramble and dense thickets of woody stems. It ends alongside cars, on a narrow lane behind the film studios. The lane fades at a curious shrine-like structure formed of concrete and girder – a marker for what? Sorrow over my failed marriage, or the silt of endless car journeys? At Fulmer they kindly give me water. By the butt I meet Grzegorz. At Pickeridge air ruffles the weeds above the gravels; rubber tubing carries water pumped from the old sandpits. A kestrel flies to the chimney of the derelict farmhouse. There are secret watercourses fenced with steel and grazed by hairy highland cattle. Looking at these I think of Jeff Nuttall[34] and the next day I run into him in the Two Jays bookshop in Edgware. Nuttall tells me he sees nature as enamel and hissing servomechanisms.

Who inhabits these towns with their purple evenings and silhouettes of poplars? I watch the blaze of traffic along the straight motor-highway over above the 'village', visit off-licences full of hostile faces to buy Tizer. It would be a quick ride back by car to known areas but walking is a different proposition; a procedure followed through darkness and cattle-dunged tracks,

---

34 *Jeff Nuttall*: artist, painter and jazz musician. His book *Bomb Culture* (1968) contained a searing attack on the then fashionable drug and hippy cultures. Died January 2004.

past barbed wire hung with tattered fleece. The war years hang heavy by the corrugated shack.

I hear the ticking of ant colonies on the brisk walk to Beaconsfield. Thoughts widen out to swans and factories, to market towns and golden larvae hidden in nettles. The Deep Library: a binding of strands or twigs – <u>fraszki</u>;[35] the pussy willow points to vast glass cities deep within the pine-kernel. The mysterious spider wobbles, all-seeing, in her web above the path by the canal.

29 VII 74

Bishop's wort
Horse-mint
Lilac-flowers[36]

I sleep out, unable to face Annette with her hair madness, her raging about Anne Aston. After a night wrapped in a horse tarpaulin, I wake to dew, to horror at proposed motorways. I turn off the canal path onto a dip leading down to a wall made of concrete strips placed horizontally into brackets. There is a section of emergent birch wood rising out of old irons. Everywhere there is a riot of red Herb Robert and the tinkle of birch leaves.

35 *Fraszki*: Polish back-formation to Latin term for bunch of twigs or sticks. Possibly a reference to the poetry of Cyprion Norwid.
36 *Bishop's wort* etc: Folk names for *Stachys officialnis* L, Betony.

These are the times I love: when <u>she</u> opens me up to the inexplicable within the imminent; when <u>she</u> enters Hillingdon and casually boards a bus. I see weld[37] grow on garage roofs. Over by the old bus station it is mullein and bedstraw. A dirty window guides the eye through mouldering frames to crinkled papers in draws and, in dark cupboards under stairs, gas bills paid in 1941.

In the railyard the ground runs down on a southward slope. Mauve moths dart ahead. This packed zone, tucked behind the crematorium, is a dirty secret. Houses line up on the other side of the railtrack. Grzegorz knew them in a dream: their effluent; their cabbages. The squeak of pram wheels ran straight through to high blood pressure in Timothy White's.[38] The million-odd trains passing up the line to Windsor Castle via Ham Island; the vinyl discs and cappuccino that shaped 1965; the cider drunk on wasteland – all of it was as nothing. And the dyer's rocket – that spotted dick of disturbance? Under the living cloud it waits as hogging is laid, picnic tables placed and cycle-tracks mapped out.

37 *Weld, dyer's rocket*: popular names for *Reseda luteola* L.; late summer plant used for centuries for the purpose of dyeing. Chaucer mentions Weld in early poem.
38 *Timothy White's*: Chain of high-street stores, similar to WH Smith. Defunct by early 1980s.

13 X 74

The fold: queen wasp clings to curtain. A weak sun warms old bones. Now rails rattle. It is alive once more. Lost in a foreign city; layers and slabs; feeders blocked by Jenny Green-Teeth.[39]

A car passed in 1960. I didn't know. I wanted mystery behind net curtains, glimpsed through crittall windows. Break-shoe is smouldering, 1946. Now our clothes are brighter. Now it is loose. Up drives; over hills.

The fold: lost stinking culverts and the hiss of changing points. Beans climb bamboo and snails sleep in rusting pipes. We have pasta and avocado pears, faces in magazines and unexercised freedoms.

The All-Seeing, hidden in hedge and shrub, beheld the fullness of garage forecourts. I saw her arrive in beautiful October. There were vast skies above the suburb. Having seen to the heart of this majesty, she then hurried home for tea and toast. June 1962: carried via intensive care far beyond the blue of school railings. Quick! There! There! Behind laurel, through fences. Among half-bricks and a plastic Red Indian sans head. The flit of moth wings against broken asbestos sheeting and fragments of orange flowerpots. The tedium of Pick of the Pops[40] recycled in turgid pubs.

39 *Jenny Green-Teeth*: Old Middlesex name for *Lemna minor* L., duckweed.
40 *Pick of the Pops*: popular BBC radio programme specialising in music from the UK singles chart. Last broadcast in 1972.

24 X 74

Today I wander up to the site of the old Hendon Greyhound Stadium.[41] There are berries of arum giving warning at the arterial road's edge. The new regional shopping centre looms like an approaching oil crisis. Later I reach Merit House,[42] where Grzegorz charts his antics in his notebooks and prints them out on his Banda: a small press in Colindale. Here I smoke and stare down at the runnelled river.

I feel troubled and bend to crawl through a holly bush nearby. A blackbird hops and then streaks away sounding his alarm. The air coils and is uneasy. Pushing past dense thickets of elder and sycamore, I see the backs of factories surround me. Mounds of freshly dumped clay and plaster edge up to the river here.

I tumble down into a culvert lined with hart's tongue and moss and am knee-deep in the current as it flows back behind me. I walk forward and exit the 1970s. I melt into mods, pass into beards and trad-jazz. I become Saxon and Jute, Roman and Briton. Eddies deepen to swirlings. Cables catch my tired feet and my spectacles slip from my nose. As I fall against the channel carrying the Tramway Ditch[43] into the Silkstream, I end.

---

41 *Hendon Greyhound Stadium*: demolished about 1974. It is now the 'Stadium Car Park' serving the Brent Cross Regional Shopping Centre.
42 *Merit House*: office block built on A5 at Colindale circa 1965, upon site of former trolley bus and tram depot, hence 'tramway ditch'.
43 *Tramway Ditch*: See footnote above. The Tramway Ditch is really two distinct streams, both of which feed the Silkstream, their confluence coinciding on opposite sides of that brook. The eastern stream rises off the side

This road curves at its exedra,[44]
Ending in rain and lit windows and then
Memories surface – not mine but <u>hers</u>.
The passing, and leaving; the search
Through outskirts for <u>her</u>,
The flap of <u>her</u> raincoat, undone.

The bark-stripped apple tree marks
The failed attempt
Buried below stubbed[45] elders
Near the cripples' training college,

Where Ver[46] rises at Kensworth
And Tiw[47] shone in conkers,

A Womere[48] accompanied by
Great flocks of birds.

---

of the Mill Hill *petit massif*, flows around the south edge of the nearby Montrose sports field and enters the Silkstream behind Merit House. The west stream flows down from Kingsbury and burrows under the A5 before surfacing to the immediate north of Merit House. It is the latter stream that seems to concern Kurland here.

44 *Exedra:* curved end of an apse.
45 *Stubbed*: possibly old Middlesex word for coppiced.
46 *Ver*: A small river in Hertfordshire.
47 *Tiw*: I have not been able to find the source or meaning of this word.
48 *Womere*: I have not been able to find the source or meaning of this word.

The Wicked Lady crouches as
The Valley of the Nightingales

Floods rapidly with
Water presaging tragedy.

After regaining high roads
Middx sheet VII just north of
Cappell Rd, running eastwards.
A butt perforated with bullet holes.
The Colne system;
The Lea system:
You spread out from here.